Lloyd George

IN THE SAME SERIES

General Editors: Eric J. Evans and P. D. King

LANCASTER PAMPHLETS

Lloyd George

Stephen Constantine

London and New York

First published in 1992 by Routledge
11 New Fetter Lane, London EC4P 4EE

Simultaneously published in the USA and Canada by Routledge
a division of Routledge, Chapman and Hall, Inc.
29 West 35th Street, New York, NY 10001

© 1992 Stephen Constantine
Printed in England by Clays Ltd,
St Ives plc

British Library Cataloging in Publication Data
Constantine, Stephen
Lloyd George.
1. Great Britain. Politics. History
I. Title
941.083092

Library of Congress Cataloguing in Publication Data
Constantine, Stephen.
Lloyd George / Stephen Constantine.
p.   cm. -- (Lancaster pamphlets)
Includes bibliographical rererences and index.
1. Lloyd George, David, 1863–1945.   2. Prime ministers--Great
Britain--Biography.   3. Great Britain--Politics and
government--1837–1901.   4. Great Britain--Politics and
government--1901–1936.   5. Great Britain--Politics and
government--1936–1945.   I. Title.   II. Series.
DA566.9.L5C66   19912
941.083'092--dc20
[B]   91-16743

ISBN 0 415 06573 9

Contents

Foreword

Lancaster Pamphlets offer concise and up-to-date accounts of major historical topics, primarily for the help of students preparing for Advanced Level examinations, though they should also be of value to those pursuing introductory courses in universities and other institutions of higher education. Without being all-embracing, their aims are to bring some of the central themes or problems confronting students and teachers into sharper focus than the textbook writer can hope to do; to provide the reader with some of the results of recent research which the textbook may not embody; and to stimulate thought about the whole interpretation of the topic under discussion.

At the end of this pamphlet is a list of works, most of them recent or fairly recent, which the writer considers most important for those who wish to study the subject further.

Chronology

1917	Struggles with Jellicoe and Haig; US declaration of war (April); Battle of Passchendaele; creates Supreme War Council (November); Corn Production Act
1918	Food rationing; German offensive (March); Maurice debate (May); Education Act; Armistice (11 November); general election (December), Coalition government continues
1919	Paris Peace Conference; Sankey Commission on coal industry; Housing Act
1920	Proposes fusion of Conservatives and Coalition Liberals (March); Welsh Disestablishment completed; Unemployment Insurance Act
1921	Economic depression and public expenditure cuts; trade treaty with Russia (March); retirement of Bonar Law (March); Irish Treaty (December)
1922	National Liberal party formed (January); Russo–German Treaty of Rapallo (April); Chanak crisis (September); Carlton Club meeting (19 October) and fall of Lloyd George; general election (November), Conservative government formed
1923	General election called by Baldwin, Liberal reunion, Conservatives lose majority (December)
1924	Labour minority government (January–October); *Coal and Power*; general election (October), Conservative government formed
1925	*The Land and the Nation; Towns and the Land*
1926	General Strike and Liberal split; succeeds Asquith as leader; Liberal Industrial Inquiry starts
1928	*Britain's Industrial Future*
1929	*We Can Conquer Unemployment*; general election (May), Labour minority government formed
1930	Lloyd George–MacDonald talks
1931	Sir John Simon leaves official Liberal party (June); Lloyd George ill (from July); National government formed (August); general election (October), Liberals split
1932	National government introduces tariffs, Liberals under Samuel reunite with Lloyd George Independent Liberals
1933	Published first volume of memoirs
1935	Council of Action for Peace and Reconstruction; General election (November), National government continues

Prologue

David Lloyd George (1863–1945) dominated the political landscape of early twentieth-century Britain. He was and remains the most successful Welsh politician of modern times. Yet he was born in Manchester: this is the first, and most explicable, of the many apparent paradoxes which enlivened his career, confused his contemporaries and perplex historians. He spent much energy publicly denouncing the aristocracy and the House of Lords, yet in 1945 he accepted a peerage and died as Earl Lloyd-George of Dwyfor: the last peculiar twist to his career.

In between he first earned a reputation as the tribune of the people, but was subsequently widely denounced as the enemy of the working class. Early in his career he posed as a Welsh nationalist, an outsider in Westminster politics, yet he advanced to become prime minister of a British government and settled in Surrey. He appeared at one period as the radical critic of the Anglican Church and of the Conservative party, too hot sometimes even for his Liberal colleagues, but he also established congenial relations with bishops and Tory leaders and proposed political coalitions and even fusion with his ostensible opponents before, during and after the First World War. Here, too, was the man who could claim to be a principal architect of Liberal revival and political domination before the First World War, and yet subsequently was deemed more responsible than any other individual for sapping Liberal morale and destroying Liberal integrity. Some observers believed him,

1

wrongly, to be a pacifist at the time of the Boer War and even in August 1914, and yet he rapidly earned a reputation thereafter as a ruthless engineer of total war and as a man who seemed ready for more armed conflict after 1918, against the Soviet Union, the Irish and the Turks. His reputation as 'The Man Who Won the War' remains for many commentators unassailable, but was he not also the man who 'lost' the peace, who failed both to secure post-war international concord and to satisfy the domestic reform expectations of the electorate which he himself had helped fuel? At one stage he struck observers as the voice of the Nonconformist conscience, yet personal scandal dogged him. He attracted an early reputation, probably fairly, as a sexual philanderer until he finally settled into a curious domesticity with a wife in Wales (Margaret) and a mistress in Whitehall (Frances Stevenson, his secretary). The sniff of financial malpractice was never far away, whether it was incompetent dealings in Patagonian goldmines, possible insider knowledge when investing in Marconi shares, or the blatant selling as prime minister of political honours to accumulate a private fund for his own political purposes. He cheerfully accepted substantial gifts from 'admirers', and on his death left £139,855, a more substantial sum than any other prime minister who took office in the first half of this century except 'Honest Stan' Baldwin, whose assets are easily traceable to the holdings of his family firm.

Not surprisingly, some of his ardent early admirers found themselves ultimately repelled by the man. Typical was Herbert du Parcq, who had written, with Lloyd George's approval and assistance, an admiring four-volume biography of the great Liberal statesman in 1911–13, but who later despaired of him and disowned the book. Also not surprisingly, even after his fall from office in 1922, Lloyd George remained a political operator who haunted the lesser men who succeeded him, such as Stanley Baldwin and Ramsay MacDonald. Baldwin, in a self-revealing phrase, described him as 'a dynamic force . . . and a dynamic force is a very terrible thing' (quoted in K. Middlemas and J. Barnes, *Baldwin*, 1969, p. 123). Baldwin's hatred of Lloyd George was remarkable even by recent political standards, driving him to deface pictures of 'the Goat' in his personal photograph album.

The discussion which follows must inevitably concentrate on certain key questions, and these are best handled within the key stages of Lloyd George's career. First, we must account for his emergence onto the national political scene and explore the extent to which he was the representative of a particularly Welsh form of Liberal radicalism. Second, we must consider his rise to prominence as a backbencher and the Liberal revival which brought the party, and Lloyd George, to power in 1905. Third, there comes his performance in government before the First World War and the passage in particular of a legislative programme which laid the basis for that social contract between government and society we call the Welfare State. Did this work improve the prospects of the party to which he was ostensibly loyal? Fourth comes the War. We must consider how he responded to the outbreak of war and the problems of mobilisation and why and with what consequences he became prime minister in 1916. Fifth, there is his conduct as leader of the post-war Coalition government. If, as has been suggested, that administration does not deserve all the criticism to which it has been traditionally subjected, how do we explain its fall in 1922, not from electoral defeat but through backbench rebellion? That leads us finally to possibly the most unexpected phase of Lloyd George's career. His fifteen years as a backbencher from 1890 to 1905 had been followed by seventeen uninterrupted years in high office until 1922, including six years as prime minister. Yet there followed a further twenty-three years in politics, always in the wilderness, as a party leader perhaps, but latterly almost without a party. Why did he never return to office, why did the vigorous intellectual and political campaigns he inspired between the wars fail to restore his personal fortunes, and how responsible was Lloyd George specifically for the increasingly dismal experiences of the Liberal party?

1

Cottage-bred man: MP for Wales, 1863–96

In 1919 the economist John Maynard Keynes, who had served with Lloyd George as a Treasury official at the Versailles Peace Conference, attempted to sum up his impressions of the man. 'How can I convey to the reader . . . any just impression of this extraordinary figure of our time, this syren, this goat-footed bard, this half-human visitor to our age from the hag-ridden magic and enchanted woods of Celtic antiquity?' (J.M. Keynes, *Essays in Biography*, 1933). This description reflected Keynes's lamentable ignorance of the United Kingdom. It owed more to his passion for Diaghilev and the Ballets Russes than to his knowledge of the world outside Cambridge and London. 'Lloyd George is rooted in nothing', he wrote. In fact, Lloyd George was rooted in Wales, and it is there that we must begin. His upbringing and experiences as a young MP were to determine his values and to affect much of his subsequent behaviour.

Lloyd George frequently referred in political speeches to his childhood and Welsh upbringing. It was a technique of personal reminiscence then rarely employed by British politicians but common among American presidents, not least two of Lloyd George's heroes, Abraham Lincoln, the former small-town lawyer, and James Garfield, whose 'log cabin to White House' career was mythologised in popular literature. Lloyd George, like his role models, was prone to trade upon his 'ordinary', even deprived, background as a way of establishing a rapport with popular

4

audiences: he could claim thereby to understand and to embody the true aspirations of everyman and everywoman. During his first election campaign in 1890 he denounced his aristocratic opponent for not realising that 'the day of the cottage-bred man has at last dawned' (quoted in Frank Owen, *Tempestuous Journey*, 1954, p. 55).

It was an effective technique because it was partly based on reality. Lloyd George was, indeed, a thoroughbred Welshman. His father, William George, came from Pembrokeshire in South Wales and his mother, Elizabeth Lloyd, from Caernarfonshire in the North. Moreover, it was a family which experienced its share of misfortunes. Lloyd George's father, like both his grandfathers, died young, only 43, when the boy Dafydd was only 1, his sister not yet 3 and his mother expecting a third child. The family was rescued by the generosity of his mother's younger brother, Richard, Uncle Lloyd, then a 30 year-old bachelor living in the tiny village of Llanystumdwy, two miles from Criccieth. Their new home, Highgate (now the Lloyd George Museum), may be described as a cottage, three rooms downstairs and two up, substantial and of stone, and with a workshop next door, but since Lloyd George's maternal grandmother also lived there it was somewhat crowded. There were times when the extended family experienced financial stress, particularly when Lloyd George was in his late teens. Certainly these were experiences rare among his later parliamentary leaders, cabinet colleagues or political opponents. This was not the childhood of Gladstone, Lord Rosebery, Balfour or Lord Curzon. Yet it seems not to have brought him closer to other men from humble backgrounds, like John Burns, Ramsay MacDonald or Ernest Bevin.

That it did not do so may be explained by a closer look at his social origins. In many respects, and particularly in the context of North Wales, David Lloyd George was a privileged child. The social categories devised to describe an industrialised English society fit uncomfortably as indicators of social class in late nineteenth-century rural Wales, but it is not straining the term too much to describe his origins as middle class, albeit of modest pretensions. His father came from a comfortable farming family, but his intellectual aspirations led him into a career as a schoolteacher. He was a somewhat peripatetic one, holding posts for example in Liverpool, in Pwllheli, where he met and married Elizabeth Lloyd, and latterly in Manchester, where David was born on 17 January 1863 in the district of Chorlton-upon-Medlock. (Predictably, Lloyd George claimed to be a Mancunian when it served his political purposes.) When David's father died he left assets worth £768, a tidy sum in those days. Moreover, the household into which the Georges were absorbed was that of an independent family firm: Richard Lloyd was a skilled shoemaker, but also an entrepreneur, employing two apprentices. There was never any question of the George boys entering anything but a professional career, if not as teachers or religious ministers then as lawyers. At some financial sacrifice, both sons became articled clerks in an important Porthmadog practice, David in 1878 and his younger brother William in 1882; both qualified as solicitors, and together they formed in 1887 their own locally-based firm, Lloyd George and George. (Lloyd George's political career increasingly left the business to be run by William, who with remarkable self-denial and considerable skill supported not only his own family but also that of his brother, at least while he remained a backbencher.) It might also be noted that David derived social prestige and some financial benefits, as well as affection and in due course five children, from his marriage in 1888 to Margaret Owen, the daughter of quite a comfortable Criccieth farming family.

When Lloyd George arrived in the House of Commons in 1890 he was, then, not without some privileges. Getting himself born in 1863 had also been a shrewd career move. It brought him to maturity when the character of the House of Commons was changing. For much of the nineteenth century, MPs, and especially ministers, had been drawn largely from the ranks of the leisured classes, usually landowners, often sons of aristocrats, who alone had the resources of time and money to support a career in Parliament. (Payment of MPs did not begin until 1911.) Admittedly lawyers had also formed a parliamentary contingent, but, from the late nineteenth century, professional society in Britain was to expand and to bring an increased number of lawyers along with businessmen into the Commons. In this respect Lloyd George was coming in on the tide.

He was privileged, too, in the intellectual and cultural environment in which he grew up. The genetically-minded might suspect that he derived some of his formidable intellectual equipment from his schoolteacher father. Certainly he inherited his books. Packed in tea chests, these had been humped up from Pembrokeshire after his father's death and crammed into the Highgate home in

6

Llanystumdwy: volumes on history, on education and on religion, plus encyclopaedias, English poetry, Shakespeare's plays and the novels of Dickens and Hugo. As a boy, Lloyd George read much of this, and with care. To this learning was added the contribution of Uncle Lloyd. Richard Lloyd was a man of local intellectual distinction, the unpaid pastor of a small Baptist sect, the Disciples of Christ or Campbellites, and his home and conversation were enriched by a wide reading of serious political and religious newspapers. The chapel itself was an intellectual stimulus which in our secular age we must not overlook. On top of this, the George children were well-taught by the local schoolteacher, David Evans, a man of rare distinction. Furthermore, as a trainee lawyer Lloyd George was drawn into the remarkably vibrant intellectual life of Porthmadog, especially centred on its debating society. Lloyd George earned no university degree, but he was no untutored son-of-the-soil. These intellectual stimuli reflected, moreover, not merely personal good fortune. The sustaining context was the deep-rooted cultural revival which blessed Wales in the second half of the nineteenth century.

Over the battlements of Caernarfon Castle fly today a Welsh Dragon and the banner of Cadw, the *Welsh* historical monuments authority. These are ambiguous flags to be seen floating above that engine of *English* imperialism, Edward I's castle. They say something about Welsh resilience, and they owe much to a Welsh cultural recovery launched particularly in Lloyd George's lifetime. The Welsh, of course, are the descendants of those Celts who had successfully resisted Anglo-Saxon invasion of the British Isles, but they had had a tough time surviving later Norman and Plantagenet penetration. Paradoxically, the coming to the English throne of the Welsh Tudors only hastened their apparent absorption into the English polity and English culture, following the Act of Union in 1536. When Lloyd George was born, Wales lacked the independent legal system, the national church and the distinctive educational practices enjoyed by Scotland. Administratively, Wales was treated as part of England, its counties governed by English law, its MPs and lords sitting in the British Parliament, its English-speaking bishops responsible to an English archbishop, enforcing the doctrines of the Anglican Communion and enjoying the privileges of the Established Church in Wales. Although most of its landowners were Welsh and resident, unlike the many absentee landlords of Ireland, they were integrated into the dominant English-speaking culture, and sent their daughters to schools modelled on English institutions and their sons to English universities. Most, like the principal landowner in Lloyd George's Llanystumdwy, could speak no Welsh. A notorious entry in a nineteenth-century edition of the *Encyclopaedia Britannica* reads 'Wales – see England'.

And yet the ingredients for a Welsh cultural and even political resurrection were not absent, and the mix became richer while Lloyd George was growing up. First, there was the language. The legal and educational efforts of the Anglican Church and English state since the time of the Tudors had failed to suppress it. (Uncle Lloyd was partially deaf because of a blow received from a teacher for speaking Welsh at school.) A parliamentary Education Commission urged its suppression in 1847 as an obstacle to progress, and thereby provoked many Welshmen to rise to its defence, for example, via the National Eisteddfod first held in 1858. In fact, the census of 1891 reveals that, out of a Welsh population of nearly 900,000, at least 55 per cent of adults were Welsh-speakers with proportions of over 90 per cent in rural Caernarfonshire and Merioneth. Many could speak only Welsh. Lloyd George himself was brought up in a Welsh-speaking home. Welsh was his first tongue; English remained a foreign language, however fluently he came to speak it. Oddly enough, whereas the very backwardness of rural Wales with its poor communications had once served to preserve the Welsh language and traditional culture, the partial modernisation of Wales in the late nineteenth century actually fostered their enrichment, partly by stimulating the development of small-town Welsh-speaking communities, like Porthmadog, led by modest middle-class businessmen and professionals, like Lloyd George, and partly by improving the means of communication, especially by cheapening the printed page. The removal of stamp duties in 1855 and paper taxes in 1861, combined with cheaper and faster printing technology, encouraged the production and wider distribution of a vast range of inexpensive Welsh-language newspapers.

Moreover, many of those Welshmen sucked into English and thereby into Western European culture could not help being affected by the tide of nationalism sweeping the nineteenth-century world. There was the excitement of Italian and German unification, the role models of Mazzini and Kossuth, even the musical inspiration of Dvorak, Smetana and Tchaikovsky. Close at hand there was the

8

example of an Irish Home Rule League, first formed in 1873, and Scotland gained its own Secretary of State in 1885.

In addition, religious Nonconformity had become well-established in Wales since the beginning of the century. Subsequent revivalism from the 1850s ensured that chapel members easily exceeded the communicants of the Anglican Church. By 1905 the latter mustered some 193,000, whereas the Nonconformists numbered over 550,000, made up particularly of Methodists, Wesleyans, Independents and Baptists. Nonconformity served as an incentive for cultural and political autonomy against the perceived tyranny of the Anglican Church and the English state, and also acted as a conduit through which cultural and political aspirations could be expressed. It followed that Nonconformity generated a conflict tantamount to a Welsh civil war. Nonconformist ministers and their intellectual and political allies among tenant farmers and the small-town bourgeoisie waged a verbal, and sometimes invoked a physical, assault upon an unholy trinity of enemies: the anglicised landowners, the Anglican clergy and their perceived allies, the brewers. Nonconformists demanded, for example, changes in the licensing laws to give greater local political control over the granting and renewal of publicans' licenses. In addition, they found repugnant the mechanism whereby the state since 1833 had helped maintain in many areas the Anglican monopoly over elementary education by granting financial subsidies to Church schools: this represented one of the ways by which the Anglican Church sought to bend the minds of the young and maintain its privileges. The most famous episode of Lloyd George's early life was when he led a schoolboy rebellion against his Anglican headteacher and the diocesan inspectors by refusing to recite the Anglican Creed. Ultimately, Nonconformists claimed, the only proper solution was the disestablishment of the Anglican Church in Wales, leaving it to compete for souls with Nonconformist chapels, preferably after prising loose its grasp of the property and other endowments it had accumulated over centuries. The Church was also buttressed by the collection of tithes, extracted by Anglican landowners from Nonconformist tenants. Objections to this exploitation were capable of being widened by radicals like Lloyd George into a wider assault on the wealth, power and prerogatives of overmighty landowners: in the 1880s, for example, only 4.2 per cent of farms in Caernarfonshire were owner-occupied, the rest being rented from landlords.

9

These campaigns required democratic political expression, and in each case the Liberal party was increasingly accepted as the vehicle to bring satisfaction. After all, the Liberal party elsewhere in the United Kingdom espoused the aspirations of Nonconformists. The cause of temperance and licensing laws had been accepted by the Liberal leadership. Gladstone had agreed to the disestablishment of the Irish Church in 1869 and had initiated major land reforms in Ireland in 1870 and 1881. And he seemed responsive to nationalist aspirations: if those of Italy, Bulgaria and Ireland, why not those of Wales?

Major electoral reforms had also made it possible at last to express popular demands and Welsh democratic aspirations through the political system. The franchise had been widened in 1867, but more important in rural Wales was the extension of the householder vote to the counties in 1884. The redrawing of constituency frontiers in 1867 and especially in 1885 also helped grassroots political opinion to become more articulate, and the secret ballot introduced in 1872, plus the Corrupt Practices Act of 1883, allowed voters to express themselves without fear or favour. Local government reforms, especially the act of 1888 which introduced electorally-accountable county councils, added further opportunities to assert local democratic opinion.

The result of these political changes at a time of religious and cultural excitement was the political transformation of Wales. The region had been notoriously a Tory stronghold through the first half of the nineteenth century, but in the election of 1868 came significant Liberal gains. Some tenants were expelled from their farms for voting the 'wrong' way by angry Tory landlords, but thereafter, protected by the secret ballot, the tide turned hugely to the Liberals. In 1880 29 of the 33 Welsh seats were captured, in 1885 30 of the 34.

Born and growing up in his social class with its vigorous democratic culture, it is not surprising that the young Lloyd George with his twitching political antennae should have embraced Welsh radical and national causes. In public speeches by the early 1880s he was attacking local Tory landlords, Anglican clergy and the demon drink. He became secretary of the local Anti-Tithe League in 1886, praised Michael Davitt, the leader of the Irish land campaign, when he came to speak locally, and rapidly earned a hot reputation as a lawyer prepared to defend the interests of Nonconformists, tenants and labourers against the presumption of parsons, squires

10

and magistrates. His energy, self-publicity and remarkably mature debating skills soon attracted the attention of local Liberals, and in the summer of 1888 he was pressed to accept nomination as the parliamentary candidate for Caernarfon Boroughs. In 1889 he was elected as an alderman by Caernarfonshire's triumphant Liberal country councillors. And in 1890, at the age of only 27, he won the by-election which launched his parliamentary career.

It was a sweet victory, defeating the Tory landowner who had been a patron of his elementary school, but not an easy one. He had a majority of just eighteen votes. The constituency was made up of six separate small towns: Caernarfon, Criccieth, Conwy, Nefyn, Pwllheli and Bangor where the Anglican cathedral brought support to his enemies. This remained a marginal constituency until 1906, and it was therefore essential for Lloyd George to attract the widest possible Liberal support: his 1890 programme, more or less repeated at the general election in 1892, was suitably vague on specifics but appropriately general in its support for such standard Welsh Nonconformist and Liberal causes as disestablishment, temperance legislation, land reform, tax changes and support for Gladstone's Irish policy.

Once in Parliament Lloyd George could not afford, nor, more importantly, did he wish, to disengage from Welsh causes. He knew he had to appear busy on behalf of Caernarfonshire constituents, and he was eager to put his considerable political energies behind the principal campaigns of Welsh Liberals. He did this certainly out of conviction during this first part of his career, but also because he believed these issues and the allies they brought him would widen his power base in Wales and guarantee his impact on Westminster politics. He joined the group of Welsh Liberal MPs under the chairmanship of Stuart Rendel (oddly enough an Englishman though representing a Welsh constituency) who demanded that Parliament should address Welsh grievances and who lobbied their party leaders and also government ministers, whether Conservative or Liberal, on behalf of Wales. Lloyd George himself first made his mark in the Commons, and in public speeches outside, by attacking publicans and demanding licensing reforms. He also condemned the Conservative government's Education Bill of 1891 for providing yet more state sustenance for Church schools, attacked as too limited their proposals for tithe reform, and mocked additional state expenditure on members of the Royal Family. He

11

rarely missed an opportunity to demand the disestablishment of the Anglican Church in Wales. Moreover, he waged verbal assault on landowners, criticising the inequities their privileges sustained and demanding land reforms: it is probable that this issue most inspired him as a young politician and for much of his later career.

However, it cannot be said that on such major matters during the 1890s much was being achieved. One obstacle was the Conservative party, in power from 1886 to 1892 and again from 1895 through to 1905. Another was Gladstone. As Liberal party leader, his preoccupation with Irish Home Rule excluded all else. Although, for example, the Liberals had officially accepted Welsh Disestablishment in 1891 as part of their programme, Gladstone cannot be seen as ever an enthusiastic convert. Even after his resignation in 1894, his successors remained reluctant to find the parliamentary time and the political energy to ram such a measure through the Commons. Besides, politicians recognised that no such change, nor other radical Welsh demands, would get past a Tory-dominated House of Lords armed with its legislative veto. Welsh Disestablishment bills were introduced in 1894 and again in 1895 but they made little parliamentary progress.

So frustrated did Lloyd George become, with Liberal colleagues as well as Tory opponents, that there came a phase when he seemed about to relaunch his career as the 'Welsh Parnell'. He had been much impressed by the single-minded discipline of the Irish parliamentary party under Charles Stuart Parnell's leadership and by its apparent ability thereby to wring reforms and concessions from Liberal and even Conservative governments. Parnell had even got the Liberals to commit themselves to Home Rule for Ireland, a constitutional revolution which would have made conceivable many other Irish domestic reforms. Lloyd George was actually unsure about Gladstonian Home Rule and rather preferred Joseph Chamberlain's more dilute form of devolution described as 'Home Rule All Round', introducing assemblies for Ireland, Scotland and – Wales. He never aspired to create a truly independent Welsh nation state, but Home Rule for Wales on either the Chamberlain or Gladstone model might allow Wales to escape from the veto on internal Welsh reform consequent upon the country's total integration into the English state. Moreover, the model of the Irish parliamentary party offered itself as the mechanism whereby Wales might extract its own concessions. A similarly tightly disciplined

12

Welsh party, suitably distanced from the national Liberal party and under dynamic leadership, preferably his own, should be capable of wresting reforms from a Westminster government.

He began to speak publicly in such a vein particularly after the 1892 election in which Welsh Liberals captured 31 of the 34 Welsh seats. The Liberal party was returned to power but with a parliamentary majority of only 40. The opportunity to exercise a bit of pressure, even a spot of blackmail, on behalf of Wales was too tempting. Dramatic steps were taken in 1894 when Lloyd George and three colleagues temporarily rejected the Liberal party whip and struck out as a bunch of independent MPs. He also schemed to combine the North Wales and the South Wales Liberal Federations and merge the lot with the popular grassroots Cymru Fydd (Young Wales) movement he had relaunched as a vehicle for Welsh national aspirations. He envisaged this unified pressure group securing the constitutional changes which would usher in Welsh land reform, disestablishment and the destruction of the Anglican and anglicised hierarchy.

It was not to be. Few of his Welsh MP colleagues were prepared to go so far so fast. Many distrusted Lloyd George's ambitions. And in truth, the interest in quasi-independence for Wales appealed more to the rural, Welsh-speaking, intensely Nonconformist North than to the more anglicised, industrial and commercial South with its intimate ties to the English economy. Lloyd George, never a political coward, attempted to capture grassroots support in South Wales behind the back of local Liberal leaders, but at a traumatic meeting in Newport on 16 January 1896 he was for once out-manoeuvred and howled down. Although he made some attempts over the succeeding months to repair the damage, he was realistic enough to recognise that this cause was lost. Effectively, the Newport meeting ended the first phase of his career.

There is in all this a danger of seeing him as merely a typical radical spokesman for Welsh Liberalism and nationalism. However, he had been able to sustain this stance convincingly in public only by concealing some of his private beliefs and behaviour. Personally, he was always an odd representative of Welsh Nonconformity. True, he remained genuinely hostile to intemperance and publicans, but as a young unmarried man, and even as a married one, he clearly regarded the official dogma of the chapel as an unacceptable guide to at least his own sexual morality. He was fortunate on several occasions that his political career did not end prematurely in scandal:

such had been the fate of contemporaries like Sir Charles Dilke and Charles Parnell.

Furthermore, in spite of Uncle Lloyd and his chapel-twice-on-Sundays (or perhaps because of it), he was in fact erratic and uncertain in his religious beliefs. As a young man he preached in chapel and even conducted, briefly, his own evangelical mission to a remote part of Caernarfonshire, but it seems very probable that in these early years his intellectual conviction in Uncle Lloyd's revealed truth withered away. Certainly there was a growing impatience with the Welsh sectarianism that threatened to split the political force of Welsh Nonconformity and for a while even kept him apart from his wife-to-be, she a Methodist, he a Baptist. He always enjoyed singing Welsh hymns and he expressed a connoisseur's appreciation of a good sermon, but mainly as theatrical events and as forms of recreation. Throughout his career he attended services when in Wales, and even in London when Margaret was in town, but there were political reasons for being seen by his constituents as still loyal to the faith. He complained peevishly, though privately, in 1890 about 'being cramped up in a suffocating malodorous chapel listening to . . . superstitions' (K.O. Morgan (ed.), *Lloyd George: Family Letters 1885–1936*, 1973, p. 35). In fact, in place of true commitment, he probably retained mainly a distant sense of a deity and a more immediate preoccupation with social improvement here and now. This question has political significance since it suggests that his support for the cause of disestablishment in Wales may have been determined less by religious conviction and more by his resentment of the social and political prerogatives of the Church. It may also explain his developing impatience with the issue and his greater interest in other radical causes.

Perhaps even more surprising was his ambivalent attitude towards Wales. As Martin Pugh puts it: 'Lloyd George's love for his Welsh homeland was of a kind that waxed strong when he was safely removed from it, and deflated with physical proximity'(Martin Pugh, *Lloyd George*, 1988, p. 6). As a young man in 1884 he dismissed Wales in his diary as 'this stinted principality'. Later, in 1908, he condemned Criccieth, rather unkindly, as 'an old gray mixed up miserable place'. Instead, as an MP he had become rapidly entranced with London, mainly as the centre of the political world to which he was devoted but also for its vibrantly exciting social life, its theatres, music halls and dinner parties and the people he could meet there. He became reluctant to face the long train

14

journey back to North Wales, even during parliamentary recesses. He began to spend even Christmas away from his family, and he would increasingly slip abroad for holidays with political friends. In particular, he discovered the Mediterranean and the south of France. Like other Celts, before and since, he turned his face with rapture to the sun. In contrast, Margaret remained devoted to Wales and to Criccieth, and her loathing of London largely explains the strains in their marriage. For long periods, particularly in the early 1890s, her husband led a bachelor's life in London, overwhelmed by loneliness and dirty washing, and a prey to temptation.

Politically, too, even as a young man and novice MP, Lloyd George's interests groped beyond Wales and the bounds of Welsh radicalism. It is arresting to discover that the young solicitor joined the Local Volunteers, learned his military drill and went on summer camps at Conwy. He hid his uniform from Uncle Lloyd. There were signs of pride in the achievements and values of the British Empire, fast-growing in his early years. Moreover, once an MP in London, he also sought out connections with English interest groups. Links were first forged with fellow Nonconformists, so we find him in London, Manchester and elsewhere addressing public meetings on temperance and on the follies of the Anglican Church: he was anxious to become known to an audience beyond Wales.

Lloyd George's upbringing and this first phase of his political career determined his values and much of his subsequent performance. It is not at all surprising, given his Welsh background, his family and his earliest political campaigning, that throughout his life he retained a strong faith in the virtues of independence and hard work. They alone had secured his own advance. These were the values of the small-town middle class, of tenant farmers, of aspiring labourers and of the chapel folk of late nineteenth-century Wales, and it was to them that Lloyd George most instinctively turned for support. It followed that he articulated their antipathy to the inherited wealth and privileges of Anglican Church and anglicised squire. For the aristocracy as a social class he reserved a particular hostility; for the monarchy he showed at best a grudging respect. Even as a young politician he was always most comfortable among self-made men, often successful entrepreneurs in industry, commerce and the media. This upbringing and these values made him less comprehending of the collectivist instincts of trade unionists and the organised labour movement.

15

We can also detect in this early phase something of Lloyd George's methods. He was always more interested in getting there than scrupulous about the route he took. He was prepared to modify his programmes to maximise his support. He also showed an early interest in using the columns of the press to extend the range of his audiences and deepen his appeal. Moreover, and most importantly, we can see his sometimes cavalier attitude towards party political loyalty and discipline. Joseph Chamberlain's social radicalism and his stance over Irish Home Rule nearly drew Lloyd George into the Liberal Unionist camp, and he was never entirely comfortable with Gladstone as leader of the Liberal party or with his successors.

The explanation lies not just in the frustration of his Welsh causes. We cannot avoid recognising the man's ambition. His ego bursts from the pages of his diary and from the early letters he sent home to Margaret from London. She had been warned during their courtship that 'My supreme idea is to get on. . . . I am prepared to thrust even love itself under the wheels of my Juggernaut' (K.O. Morgan (ed.), *Lloyd George: Family Letters 1885–1936*, 1973, p. 14). There was never any question in his mind of remaining a country solicitor or, once elected to Parliament, of mouldering as a modest backbencher. His agitation on behalf of Welsh causes was partly fired by the determination to make a name for himself in national politics. The united Welsh mass movement he attempted to forge under his personal leadership was intended to be a vehicle for advancing the cause of Lloyd George as well as of Wales. This is not to impute to him any hypocrisy, merely to suggest that his personal and political expectations probably always exceeded the aspirations of most Welsh Liberals. The satisfaction of their goals would still have left him with other ambitions. As it transpired, Welsh objectives were only partially realised in this period: indeed, Welsh Disestablishment was only finally implemented in 1920. Long before then Lloyd George had grown frustrated by failures and impatient with merely Welsh causes. Signs of this became visible early in the next stage of his career.

2
Radical backbencher, 1896–1905

After his setback at Newport in 1896, Lloyd George set out more vigorously to cultivate for himself the posture of a national figure in British politics and to secure his entry into mainstream Liberal counsels. This was never going to be easy. His efforts to construct a Welsh Liberal party had left him with the reputation in Westminster as still an outsider, an exotic provincial lobbying for peculiarly Welsh reforms and a Liberal of doubtful loyalty to his leaders. To satisfy his ambitions Lloyd George needed on the one hand to 'escape' from Wales and extend his appeal by embracing major British and not just Welsh concerns. However, on the other hand he needed to retain his power base in Wales, not only because that was the location of his constituency but because he expected his leadership of a considerable body of Welsh Liberal supporters to give him some clout in the counsels of the party. The tricky bit was to extend his range without losing his first supporters. Moreover, he had no taste to remain a mere backbencher; he aspired to ministerial office. But such elevation was dependent upon a resurrection of the Liberal party at a time when some were even beginning to doubt its long-term future.

Lloyd George never seriously considered shifting constituencies, even though Caernarfon Boroughs was for some time a marginal seat. He was never an enthusiastic constituency MP. In between elections he tended to leave much of the local party organisation, the nursing of his constituents and the 'kissing of babies' to the care

17

of his wife, his brother and other loyal workers. But like all MPs, he was expected to defend constituency interests by energetic speech-making in the House of Commons and by judicious lobbying of ministers behind the scenes. Lloyd George not only obtained 'rewards' for his constituency – for example, a central government subsidy for Caernarfon's waterworks and approval for a light railway to Nefyn – but he ensured that constituents knew what he had accomplished: at the election in 1900 he had his deeds publicised in the local press.

Moreover, he could not afford to abandon his contacts with Wales as a whole. After the upset of 1896 he made no serious attempt to take command of the Welsh Liberal parliamentary group, even when the chairmanship fell vacant in 1898, recognising the distrust he had generated among some of his colleagues and no longer seeing such a role as helpful to his interests. But he maintained for a while his involvement with Cymru Fydd and succeeded in 1898 in establishing and leading at least one all-Wales talking shop, the Welsh National Liberal Council. Furthermore, he took up in Parliament in the later 1890s those issues which attracted particular Welsh attention, such as the 1896 report of the Royal Commission on Land in Wales, the notorious Penrhyn Quarry lockout and the Conservative government's Voluntary Schools Bills of 1896 and 1897 which proposed yet more state financial support for struggling (and mainly Anglican) Church schools.

However, in these same years he also widened his contacts and enhanced his reputation in British politics by taking a prominent part in national British controversies. For example, he sustained a long and dazzling opposition to the Conservatives' Agricultural Land Rating Bill of 1896. This purported to be a sensible measure, recommended by a Royal Commission, to provide some financial relief from the agricultural depression. Lloyd George denounced the scheme to reduce by half the rates levied on agricultural land as a dishonest attempt to lighten the taxes on privileged landowners at the expense of the productive classes. He had much fun in the House of Commons calculating how much Cabinet ministers would personally benefit from their disinterested legislation: for example, the Duke of Devonshire, Lord President of the Council, would save a comforting £10,000. Lloyd George also secured his membership in 1899 of a House of Commons Select Committee on the Aged Deserving Poor. Previous official inquiries had cautiously investigated old age pensions: on this occasion, and partly due to

Lloyd George's prodding, the committee recommended a non-contributory scheme. This was not the first, but it was the most public, demonstration of Lloyd George's growing concern for social conditions.

Since 1896 Lloyd George had therefore made some progress, making his mark in the Commons, deepening his involvement in wider national issues, while still maintaining his power base in Wales. But it was a strategy fraught with difficulties, as the Boer War beginning in October 1899 revealed.

Ever since the British occupation of the Cape Colony during the Napoleonic Wars, the security of Britain's interests in southern Africa had been a major anxiety for imperial governments. Bitter relationships between British settlers and the dispossessed Dutch or Boers were compounded by clashes with the Zulus. Political and military conflicts had bruised all these communities. Only an uneasy stability endured in the early 1880s between the British in Cape Colony and Natal and the Boers in the republics of the Transvaal and the Orange Free State. That balance was upset later in the decade by the discovery of gold in the Boer territories. Such wealth threatened to enhance enormously the economic and therefore political clout of the Boer republics in southern Africa at the expense of Cape Colony and British imperial paramountcy. Moreover, the discoveries excited the covetous gaze of British and foreign speculators and colonial settlers, and a flood of prospectors and entrepreneurs muscled over the frontiers, to the consternation of the Boers. In an attempt to maintain their political control, the Boer governments restricted the voting rights of these alien *uitlanders* and thereby provided the British authorities with the excuse to condemn President Kruger and his colleagues. Joseph Chamberlain, Secretary of State for the Colonies in the Conservative government formed in 1895, combined with Sir Alfred Milner, the British High Commissioner in South Africa, to increase the pressure. The Jameson Raid in December 1895 was a farcical attempt to seize control via a *coup d'état*: the Boer War of 1899–1902 was its tragic corollary.

The war polarised British public opinion. Most serious was its divisive impact upon Liberal supporters, even among Nonconformists and not least among the Welsh. Anti-militarists, internationalists and anti-imperialist Little Englanders condemned British policy as a violation of their pacifist, Christian and Liberal principles. But probably a majority of the population including many Liberal voters were at least initially swayed by imperial and patriotic rhetoric and were persuaded that the war was just or necessary. Between the extremes were those who certainly took some pride in Britain's global supremacy and her imperial mission but who believed her moral influence and her reputation for justice would be damaged by aggressive action against small nations. Some people in this group might have found it hard to appear unpatriotic by opposing the war, but they were suspicious of its origins and became increasingly dismayed by the methods used to wage it.

Lloyd George largely belonged to the last category, although his fierce condemnation of the government brought him into alliance with critics in the first. Whatever his opponents and sometimes his less perceptive admirers claimed, he was not a pacifist nor a Little Englander nor in general an anti-imperialist. As noted, as a young man he had shown flickers of pride in the magnitude and achievements of the British Empire (and of Wales's contribution), he had not opposed the Liberal government's advance into Uganda in 1893 and he had even condemned Salisbury for truckling to the Americans in the Venezuela crisis in 1896. But nor was he an uncritical imperialist. Some historians have stressed how he admired in turn Joseph Chamberlain and Lord Rosebery. However, Lloyd George's approval was largely for their professed commitment to social reform at home rather than for the imperial expansion overseas which they, but not Lloyd George, appeared to regard as a prerequisite. In fact, prior to the Boer War, he had not shown much sustained interest in international affairs.

He condemned the war partly on principle. From his Welsh Baptist background he drew the certainty that war was terrible: it should therefore only ever be undertaken as a last resort and only in a just cause. But there was, he claimed, no justice in the British case. It was not being fought, as officially stated, to establish the democratic rights of *uitlanders*. Kruger had in fact offered concessions which would in time establish the right of residents to vote, and this would secure British interests by peaceful means. He condemned too those with vulgar commercial interests in war, in particular greedy South African capitalists, often Jews (a vein of anti-semitism tainted many radical critiques of the war). Lloyd George also correctly claimed that Chamberlain's family businesses had greatly profited from government war contracts. He was also appalled by the increasingly brutal ways in which the war was fought, especially the concentration camps for women

20

and children. This war, he argued, was damaging Britain's good reputation, not least as a civilised and benevolent imperial nation. It threatened to unite other great powers against Great Britain and thus render more insecure an Empire which it was supposed to strengthen.

Moreover, and for Lloyd George perhaps most seriously, the war distracted attention, deliberately, from domestic problems. Chamberlain was spending on the destructive business of war the resources which should have been invested in constructive social reform: 'There was not a lyddite shell which burst on the African hills that did not carry away an Old Age Pension' (quoted in Martin Pugh, *Lloyd George*, 1988, p. 23). In addition, Lloyd George saw in the war, its costs and its casualties a weapon with which to assault the Conservative party. Initially the war was widely popular and the Conservatives did, indeed, recapture lost seats in the 'Khaki' election of October 1900. But there was no way, he knew, by which the Liberal party and therefore Lloyd George could gain power at the expense of the Conservatives by being *more* imperialist and *more* enthusiastic for the war than government supporters. Hence political calculation as well as morality inspired his sustained and brilliant campaign against the Boer War and the Conservative government.

His attacks mainly took the form of newspaper articles and especially of speeches in Parliament and on public platforms up and down Great Britain. To criticise the war and to express what were undoubtedly minority opinions to often very hostile audiences took much political and indeed physical courage. This may have been his finest hour. Politics at the turn of the century was a rough old business. He was physically attacked at meetings in Glasgow and in Liskeard in Cornwall, and it required remarkable spirit to try to address a meeting in December 1901 in Birmingham, Joseph Chamberlain's political territory: a crowd of at least 30,000 tried to storm the building, bottles and bricks (some wrapped in barbed wire) were hurled at the platform, a policeman and one of the demonstrators were killed and Lloyd George escaped with his life only by being smuggled away disguised as a constable.

These speeches and adventures brought their political rewards. Lloyd George had become news. Crucially, he had secured fruitful contacts with important political forces outside Wales, in particular with anti-war Nonconformists in England. The link with the Quaker businessman George Cadbury was additionally useful,

21

because Cadbury provided much of the cash which helped a syndicate involving Lloyd George to purchase the *Daily News*. Overnight that organ was transformed from a pro-war into an anti-war newspaper and, more particularly, one which supported Lloyd George. Moreover, he had now become a man much favoured by the National Liberal Federation, which represented constituency opinion. In brief, his reputation as a national politician was established. By the time the war was over he was being tipped for high office.

But no gains without pains. Lloyd George's high profile and individualist campaign against the war inevitably exacerbated the difficulties within the Liberal party leadership where the divisions within public opinion were alarmingly reflected. On the one hand were idealists like John Morley who condemned the war as incompatible with the principles of Liberal pacifism and internationalism. On the other were outright supporters of the war whose views brought them perilously close to the Conservatives: these were the Liberal Imperialists like Grey, Haldane, Asquith and Rosebery. In between was Campbell-Bannerman, the nominal party leader, reluctant to condemn the war but increasingly antagonised by the way it was being fought: it was he who coined the devastating phrase 'methods of barbarism'. What he lacked was the authority to impose discipline upon the party. Lloyd George's views naturally sometimes lifted the hearts of the pacifist wing, but he was reluctant to see even the Liberal Imperialists lost to the party. He had much in common with and some respect for Campbell-Bannerman, but he doubted his capacity to unite and lead the party and sometimes publicly expressed his concern in abrasive criticisms. It cannot be said that Lloyd George caused the splits in the party hierarchy, and he behaved far less outrageously than the Liberal Imperialists, but he did not succeed in improving upon his earlier reputation as a man of doubtful party loyalty.

Perhaps more dangerous was the risk Lloyd George ran during the war of losing his Welsh power base. As noted, Welsh opinion was divided by the issue, South Wales with its industrial and commercial interests being particularly susceptible to the appeal of Empire. Even in Criccieth, Lloyd George's family were exceptional as 'pro-Boers': indeed, Lloyd George, his brother and even Uncle Lloyd were burnt in effigy by local patriots. He confronted and apparently won round a hostile audience in Nefyn, but in Bangor after one stormy meeting in April 1900 local roughs nearly terminated his career with a bludgeon, bashing in his top hat and nearly his head. In the general election of 1900 his majority crept up to only 296, giving him a mere 53 per cent of the vote compared to an average for all Welsh Liberals of 58.5 per cent. Fortunately for Lloyd George's political future, opinion in Wales as elsewhere thereafter tended to swing against the government. In the event, Lloyd George came out of the war with his power base in Wales secure, with his reputation elsewhere in Britain enhanced and with his skull still intact.

It is probable that the risks he had run over the Boer War explain Lloyd George's more circumspect, even devious, response to the next major political rumpus he entered. Balfour's Education Bill of 1902 proposed, first, to legalise state secondary schools, second, to transfer responsibility for elementary schools from the locally-elected school boards created in 1870 to education committees of county, county borough and large borough or urban district councils and, third and most controversial, to provide local ratepayers' money as subsidies to schools run by voluntary bodies in return for some education committee supervision. In England and Wales in 1901 there were some 2.6 million children under 12 attending 5,700 board schools, where their religious education was blandly non-denominational, but 3 million children went to 14,000 (obviously smaller) voluntary schools, mainly controlled by the Church of England. Moreover, some 1 million Nonconformist children were educated in about 8,000 parishes where the only school was Anglican.

Lloyd George at first saw merit in the bill's proposal to develop the nation's schools by making their management a responsibility of local councils and by guaranteeing their proper funding and supervision. He recognised the crucial need for educational improvements in a more competitive world. Moreover, he had no objection to some religious education and did not seek the kind of secular state education demanded by some radicals. Besides, he seems to have become tired of these distracting sectarian conflicts. But he was soon reminded that public funding of Anglican schools without taking full public control of their staffing and curriculum remained repugnant to Nonconformist opinion in England and, of course, in Wales. Here was an issue which as a Welsh radical with a public record of opposition to Church schools and Anglican privilege he could scarcely evade, and at least it provided one more stick with which to beat the Conservatives. Once more he took to the road, denouncing the measure in public speeches

23

up and down the country as well as fighting the bill clause by clause in Parliament. This might, of course, serve politically to cement his ties with Nonconformist opinion in England, but in practice he was forced to identify most closely with the Welsh. Whereas Nonconformists in England were in a minority and could mark their opposition to the Act, once passed, only by breaking the law and withholding their rates, Nonconformists formed the majority in Wales, and their resentment could be expressed by the opposition of democratically-elected Liberal councils to the implementation of (English) national law. Once Lloyd George came to lead the resistance, this was the strategy he recommended. The opportunities for frustrating the Education Act were considerable, and they provoked the Conservatives in 1904 into threatening councils with the Education (Local Authority Default) Act, known locally as the 'Coercion of Wales' Act.

But although hugely successful in uniting Welsh Liberals against the law, Lloyd George clearly feared that a political consequence might be to confine him once more to the role of MP for Wales, a provincial figure in British politics. Coupled to his sneaking sympathy for the Act's educational purposes, this was sufficient to persuade him to seek a way out. The technique attempted was to become, regrettably, characteristic of his style. He paralleled his public denunciations with private negotiations, inflaming public controversy while seeking private compromise. In 1903–4 his overtures were to the Bishop of St Asaph, ostensibly a representative of the enemy but, so Lloyd George discovered, a kindred spirit in his desire for a settlement. In truth, neither party could control his rampant supporters. Lloyd George was obliged to back off lest he lose his Welsh power base. This at least he retained, and it was to do him no harm when a Liberal government was later being formed. Opposition to the Education Act, however, rumbled on even after the resignation of the Conservatives late in 1905.

One further disadvantage to Lloyd George flowing from this preoccupation was that it left him with less time to engage with his preferred enemy, Joseph Chamberlain, over the issue of tariff reform. This was the subject which dominated politics in England, whatever was happening in Wales, from May 1903 when Chamberlain launched his campaign. Asquith rather than Lloyd George became the pre-eminent critic of Chamberlain's proposal that Britain should abandon the principles of free trade and seek her welfare through a system of tariff protection plus imperial preferences. This project was an amazing bonus for a formerly fractured Liberal party. It is difficult to believe that Lloyd George shared the kind of religious faith in free trade enjoyed by Gladstonians, but he knew a gift when he saw one, seized it with glee, and cheerfully assaulted Chamberlain's dream, whenever he could, in public and parliamentary speeches. Moreover, his involvement over an issue around which the Liberals were reuniting secured his place among the leaders of the party.

The Liberal party needed his energy. British politics at the turn of the century were dominated by the Conservative party. They had capitalised on the electoral transformation in England after 1885 which gave them so many secure suburban as well as English rural seats; they had benefited from the growth of a lower-middle-class electorate; their party coffers had been flooded with funds from wealthy new urban supporters, many fleeing 'dangerous' Liberalism; their constituency organisation had been improved and deepened socially by the remarkable nationwide spread of the party's Primrose League; and they had earned a reputation for sound administration, sensible reforms and the firm defence of British interests in the Empire and in Ireland.

Meantime, the Liberals had been in difficulties. The loss of the Whig elite during the Home Rule crisis in the late 1880s may have helped their image as a popular democratic party, but they certainly suffered from the simultaneous departure of radicals like Chamberlain. Moreover, Gladstone's longevity and preoccupation with the Irish question had left frustrated many Liberals who wished to see the party direct its reforming impulses towards other issues, like Nonconformist rights, temperance legislation, municipal activities, constitutional changes, land reforms, the na-tionalist aspirations of Scotland and Wales, labour legislation and social welfare. The famous Newcastle programme agreed at a party conference in 1891 listed these distinctive yet competing sectional enthusiasms: the Liberals risked becoming a party of 'faddists', an umbrella for protest movements. Furthermore, the brief Liberal administration of 1892–5 exposed how few of those commitments could be realised while Gladstone remained prime minister and the House of Lords retained both its veto and its Conservative majority. The departure of Gladstone in 1894 hardly improved matters so long as so many Liberals remained loyal to his causes and so long as no senior figure acquired his prestige as leader. An unhappy period followed. Rosebery's vacillating

25

commitment to being the new leader and his attempts to alter party priorities distressed many Liberals. Disaffection also faced his eventual successor, Harcourt, who grumpily resigned as leader in 1898. The Liberals had been trounced in the election of 1895 (177 Liberal MPs to 411 Conservatives and Liberal Unionists), clawed back some ground in subsequent by-elections, but were still left way behind in 1900 (184 seats to the government's 402). Some indication has been given of the Boer War controversies which exacerbated Campbell-Bannerman's troubled inheritance: there were conspiracies to depose him, involving Asquith, Grey and Haldane, but none, it is worth stressing, by Lloyd George.

Yet in December 1905 Balfour's Conservative government resigned, and Campbell-Bannerman became prime minister. He stuffed the mouths of his principal critics with offers of high office, and went on to lead the Liberals to a resounding general election victory in January 1906 (Liberals 400 seats, Conservatives and Liberal Unionists 157).

In truth, this was largely an election which the government lost rather than one the opposition won. Substantial sections of the electorate had been alienated by the prolonged and disturbing nature of the Boer War (and the rise in taxes to pay for it), the immigration of Chinese labourers to restore cheaply the South African economy (denounced as 'Chinese slavery'), the favourable treatment of voluntary schools by the Education Act (offending Nonconformists), a new Licensing Act in 1904 (irritating temperance reformers) and especially the controversial tariff reform campaign (splitting even Conservative loyalists). Chamberlain's resignation from the government in 1903 and Balfour's sacking of extremist free traders left the government and its party in disarray.

It cannot be claimed that Lloyd George was responsible for their confusion. He was, however, one of the leading Liberal politicians who, scenting blood, seized upon the obvious opportunities to hound and harry the Conservatives first into resignation and then into electoral massacre. It was remarkable how little the Liberals needed to offer the electorate by way of positive Liberal programmes. Most of their election material concentrated on attacking Conservative errors. Much of the rest promised protection to traditional Liberal supporters – Nonconformists, temperance reformers, respectable trade unionists. Constructive social reform may have become the ambition of some younger Liberals, but it remained a sub-theme, even in Lloyd George's campaign.

However, what he had personally ensured since the turn of the century was that he would be campaigning as a cabinet minister. He had managed, after all, to maintain his balance. On the one hand, he had retained the loyalty of his power base in Wales through the difficulties of the Boer War and the twists and turns of the education controversy: the Welsh and Lloyd George formed an interest group it would be unwise of a new prime minister to ignore. On the other hand, Lloyd George had also considerably extended his appeal to English radicals, especially among Nonconformists, by his vigorous opposition to such Conservative legislation as the Agricultural Land Rating Bill, by his increasingly respected stance over the Boer War, by his opposition to Anglican privilege in education and latterly by his defence of the principle of free trade. He had ceased to be notorious and had become famous. When Campbell-Bannerman constructed his cabinet, Lloyd George could not be excluded, and he was made President of the Board of Trade. He was 42.

3

New Liberal,
1906–14

The general election of 1906 brought both opportunities and challenges to the new Liberal government. After so long a period in opposition the Liberals had at last the chance to make an enduring impact on the nation and to secure perhaps their long-term pre-eminence by the quality of their administration and by constructive legislation. However, the size of their parliamentary majority was not indefinitely secure nor, indeed, an unmixed blessing. The Conservative opposition in the House of Commons was tiny, but the first-past-the-post electoral system had exaggerated the Conservative party's fall from favour. They had still attracted 43.6 per cent of the vote, so the basis for a recovery remained. Moreover, the Conservatives dominated that extraordinary relic from the past, the unreformed House of Lords, armed with its constitutional right to veto House of Commons legislation. In addition, some observers detected potential trouble for the Liberal party in the arrival of a substantial bloc of 30 Labour party MPs, even though all but five of these new members had been returned unopposed by the Liberals thanks to a pact to share out constituencies, negotiated between the two parties in 1903. There were also the 83 Irish Nationalists who were unlikely to let the Liberal cabinet forget old obligations. And finally trouble might even be expected from the Liberal backbenches, exulting in their unexpected numbers, fired by a determination to see their particular missions fulfilled and baying for instant government action. Among the Liberal MPs were 177

Nonconformists, the largest number to sit in the Commons since the parliaments of Oliver Cromwell.

This situation brought similar opportunities and challenges to Lloyd George. He had achieved his current status as a formidable critic of governments, but we should not exaggerate his practical achievements. He had not, for example, actually brought about an early end to the Boer War nor had he forced a withdrawal of the Education Act. There had been no disestablishment of the Anglican Church in Wales, no Home Rule for Wales, no savage reduction in licensed drinking and no significant land reforms. But his activities had raised expectations among his Nonconformist and radical followers, particularly in Wales. It was now time for the destructive critic to prove himself a constructive legislator and administrator. Personally, he wished to leave his mark politically while in office, and he was aware that success would sustain his rise to more senior positions. However, if he could not satisfy the expectations of his original supporters, he would have to secure himself by extending still further the bases of his political appeal.

By 1906 he had clearly established a reputation beyond Wales and even beyond the ranks of Nonconformists throughout Britain. Moreover, as noted, he had displayed some impatience over the years with the priorities and narrow preoccupations of many of his most fervent admirers. Nevertheless, his power base in Wales was one that, for both personal and political reasons, he had no wish to lose. At least he now enjoyed an apparently untroubled ascendancy in his constituency of Caernarfon Boroughs. In the 1906 election he was able to spend most of his time campaigning on behalf of colleagues and still achieve a massive majority of 1,224: not until much later when the prospect of an election loomed up in 1945 was his security of tenure again in doubt. Moreover, throughout Wales he was able to capitalise upon his prestige as a member of the cabinet and apparently as the first truly Welsh minister of the Crown since the days of King James I. He continued to attend meetings of Welsh MPs, if only to monitor their behaviour, and he sought out prestigious offices which would undemandingly maintain his reputation in Wales: for example, serving as president of the Welsh National Liberal Council and in 1908–9 as president of the Welsh Baptist Union (whose business he insisted must be conducted in Welsh) and becoming the formal chairman of Caernarfonshire County Council. He even got himself made Constable of Caernarfon Castle in 1908 and then in 1911 sponsored in that glorious setting the investiture of the Prince of Wales. On the same lines he always tried to attend the annual National Eisteddfod, with the status of archdruid, drummed up royalty to open major events and public buildings in Wales (like Cardiff Docks) and, as ever, cultivated the Welsh press. Furthermore, at the Board of Trade he could satisfy some local demands by assisting the development of Welsh ports, railways and other economic activities. He also secured for Wales in 1907 the establishment of a separate Welsh Department at the Board of Education, the first bureaucratic creation since the Act of Union to recognise the distinctive interests of Wales. He followed up this model in 1911 when he created the Welsh National Insurance Commission. These gestures to Welsh nationalism also provided Lloyd George with useful opportunities for exercising patronage in Wales: new government jobs for Welshmen were being created and appointments had to be made.

But many Welsh people and Nonconformists nationally were looking for more than gestures, showmanship and press releases. They demanded, for example, a new Education Act to remove the privileges of voluntary schools recently confirmed in the 1902 Act, and they expected Lloyd George in office to remain their champion. It was a duty which he was obliged to accept but reluctant to perform. He knew that the House of Lords would never approve the amending legislation the Nonconformists desired. The Liberal Education Bill of 1906, bearing in its specifically Welsh proposals the stamp of Lloyd George, was actually a pretty misshapen and ill-thought-out measure even before the amendments of the House of Lords in effect reversed its intentions and forced its withdrawal. Moreover, he also came to realise what Nonconformists would not appreciate, that the issue was not one upon which the Liberal government could risk a fresh appeal to the country. This early failure disillusioned many Liberal supporters and cast some doubt on his credibility.

Also tricky was the related demand that something at last should be done to disestablish the Anglican Church in Wales. Once again, this was a priority to which the Liberal leadership and Lloyd George in particular had long been committed. Unfortunately, it was a subject which now frankly bored him and which was losing some of its potency even in Wales, not least because of improvements in the quality and conduct of the Anglican Church. Besides, this was another issue which would make no progress against the stubborn veto of the House of Lords. Typically he sought a way out by discreet negotiation, proposing in 1906 a Royal Commission (a well-known stalling tactic) and suggesting a form of disestablishment which would leave the Church with virtually all its financial and material assets (except tithes). Outraged Welshmen in response attempted to stage a revolt, remarkably reminiscent of Lloyd George's behaviour as a backbencher in 1894–6. But Lloyd George the minister demonstrated his mastery over Wales by attending the critical mass meeting, a Nonconformist convention in Cardiff in October 1907: those delegates he had not 'nobbled' beforehand were either bought off by the promise of an eventual Disestablishment Bill or were drowned in his oratory: 'Duw a wyr mor anwyl yw Cymru lan i mi!' (God knows how dear to me is my Wales!) (quoted in Peter Rowland, *Lloyd George*, 1975, p. 193). He wept, and so did they. A Disestablishment Bill was indeed introduced in 1909, but he was barely involved, the Lords remained ready with their veto and the government let the proposal be shunted aside by more pressing business.

In somewhat similar fashion, Lloyd George accepted the need for the Liberal government to frame a new Licensing Bill to appease temperance reformers among the party rank and file. However, he feared that a severe measure would dangerously alienate working-class electors, and he had lost interest in the consequent bill even before it was ritually slaughtered by the Lords in 1908. By that time he was immersed in other things. His movement away from traditional Liberal preoccupations was accelerating, and his status and political eminence became even less dependent on Wales and Nonconformity.

As President of the Board of Trade, Lloyd George's constructive achievements enhanced enormously his reputation in the cabinet, in Parliament, in the Liberal party and in the country. Indeed, he was undoubtedly one of the more successful ministers in Campbell–Bannerman's troubled government of 1906–8. The Board of Trade had changed over the nineteenth century, losing some responsibilities with the coming of free trade but gaining others. In so far as the state retained obligations for the orderly running of the capitalist economy, many duties were concentrated here. For example, it supervised industrial relations, though in the past cautiously and reluctantly. However, when a national rail strike was threatened in 1907 Lloyd George acted with remarkable energy and much cunning to bring about a settlement. Even the King, uncharacteristically, was full of praise. Then there were

31

his legislative successes, particularly the Merchant Shipping Act (1906), the Census of Production Act (1906), the Patents and Designs Act (1907), the Companies Amendment Act (1907) and the Port of London Authority Act (1908). Their significance was fourfold. First, although these Acts owed much to earlier inquiries and departmental briefings, Lloyd George prepared their details by consulting on an unprecedented scale many of those whose interests would be most deeply affected, for example, shipowners, industrialists and dock company managers: many of those formerly hostile to the Welsh radical were pleasantly surprised to find him a man with whom they could do business. And thus his political admirers grew. Second, these extended contacts increased his sympathy for entrepreneurs in general. Thereafter in his career he was to turn repeatedly for advice and help to such men. The obverse was some scepticism of the expertise and advice of civil servants. Third, his dealings as a minister with interest groups increased his preference for private negotiations rather than open political debate as a way of resolving issues. Fourth, and most important, he derived from his legislative and equally from his administrative experiences a vivid appreciation of the potential power of the state. His critics sometimes argued that his measures were serious departures from the principles of free trade and non-interference by the state. For example, the Merchant Shipping Act imposed safety obligations on foreign vessels trading into British ports and thereby protected British companies against unfair competition. Lloyd George was unmoved: the gospel of *laissez-faire* gave way to pragmatic support for what he regarded as British interests. Thus accelerated that shift towards a more positive relationship between government and society which was to be the most characteristic and potent legacy of his long period in power.

Such success as he enjoyed was some compensation at this time for the most severe personal tragedy of his life, the death on 29 November 1907 of his eldest daughter Mair, aged 17. Some have claimed that his grief was the spur which thereafter drove him forward as a social reformer. In reality, until now it had been opportunity not motive that he lacked, and the former came in April 1908. Campbell–Bannerman was dying, and Asquith, the Chancellor of the Exchequer, replaced him as prime minister. In the cabinet reshuffle, Lloyd George's credentials, as a successful minister and as a politician with a remarkable personal following in Wales and outside, ensured his promotion. Asquith also needed a man of the left in a senior post to balance his cabinet. Lloyd George was made chancellor. His enhanced status gave him the chance to use constructively the state's authority to raise revenue and to direct government expenditure.

Evidence of Lloyd George's concern for social conditions in urban and rural Britain can be traced right back to his earliest political pronouncements, but his knowledge and commitment had undoubtedly been further fuelled by the very considerable public discussions of such matters around the turn of the century. Perceptions of the extent and causes of poverty had been sharpened by the work of social investigators like Seebohm Rowntree, whose *Poverty, a Study of Town Life*, published in 1901, was a text to which Lloyd George frequently referred. Such studies confirmed the claims of radical social critics and even disturbed the complacency of many middle-class observers. Moreover, the consequences of social distress were vividly revealed by the apparent physical and mental inadequacies of the working classes when faced by overseas industrial competitors or even military rivals: the Boer War, for example, had exposed the awful quality of many of the young men who had volunteered to fight. So-called New Liberalism was the ideology of many, particularly younger, Liberal politicians like Winston Churchill and Liberal intellectuals such as L.T. Hobhouse who wished to see the party escape the restrictions of Gladstonian economics and rigid adherence to *laissez-faire* (and the obsession with Home Rule) and embrace the challenge of devising effective state welfare reforms. Their programme instinctively appealed to Lloyd George: he declared in 1908 that sickness and unemployment were 'problems with which it is the business of the State to deal'.

To what extent did Lloyd George propose Liberal social reforms in response to the emergence of the Labour party and in order to forestall its future growth? He was certainly aware that the Labour party was using the need for social improvements in order to attract recruits. He also knew that the Liberal party could not merely assume the continued allegiance of working-class voters. In an important public speech in 1906 he argued that if the government failed to address social problems Labour would indeed become 'a great and sweeping force in this country – a force that will sweep away Liberalism' (quoted in B.B. Gilbert, *David Lloyd George*, 1987, p. 290). And the loss of by-elections to Labour that year reminded him that the Liberals had to keep on their toes. Nevertheless, at this time of his career, Lloyd George remained confident that Labour could be retained as a junior partner in a progressive alliance aimed at the Conservatives.

The major political incentive to take up the cause of Liberal social reform was the continuation of Chamberlain's tariff reform campaign and the growing commitment of the Conservatives to it. Lloyd George was acutely sensitive to its potential popular appeal, even after a severe stroke in 1906 left its principal inspiration a stumbling and mumbling invalid. Chamberlain had offered a constructive vision of improved imperial defence, greater national prosperity, more security of employment and higher standards of living. Moreover, new customs duties on imports would provide government with the revenue to finance extended measures of public welfare: the need for social reform was recognised by the political right as well as the left. Lloyd George was sure that even after their recent electoral victory the Liberals needed to offer an attractive alternative to tariff reform. By 1908 this was urgent. The Liberal government could point to few constructive achievements likely to enthuse their supporters and maintain their electoral appeal, and the veto of the House of Lords was an insufficient excuse. There was only a handful of promising domestic measures – an industrial injuries act, school meals for necessitous children and a trade union law (in fact a Labour proposal) in 1906, school medical inspection in 1907, and the securing of the eight-hour working day for miners in 1908 – but little else. By-elections lost to the Conservatives indicated an Opposition revival. Lloyd George concluded in May 1908 that 'It is time we did something that appealed straight to the people . . . to stop the electoral rot' (quoted in William George, *My Brother and I*, 1958, p. 220).

The Old Age Pensions Act of 1908 was the first social reform measure which Lloyd George steered through Parliament in his new guise as a social reforming chancellor. Curiously, although he later cheerfully accepted the credit when it proved to be popular, the Act was neither of his devising nor did he fully approve of its terms. Asquith had drawn up an ambitious pensions scheme before becoming prime minister. Although initially hedged around with restrictions to limit benefits only to the 'deserving poor' and to those over 70, these non-contributory pensions rapidly proved massively more expensive to the government (and taxpayer) than Asquith had calculated. Previously Lloyd George had publicly supported pensions for the elderly, but as chancellor he faced the immediate problem of raising the necessary revenue to pay for them. But there was more. He also had to find the money to equip the Royal Navy with hugely expensive Dreadnought battleships: he was reluctantly persuaded that this was a necessary response to Germany's naval expansion.

These financial obligations confirmed for most Conservatives the inevitability of tariff reform. They argued that only indirect taxes, particularly customs duties paid for by all consumers, could raise the necessary revenue. The Liberals, however, had a proud history of reducing indirect taxes, especially on food imports, since they necessarily hit the poor most severely; hence their commitment to free trade. However, Gladstone had also argued that direct taxation, particularly income taxes, should be used only rarely and sparingly. Traditionally, then, the only financial option for Liberals was to limit government expenditure so as to allow all forms of taxation to be kept low. Lloyd George and most (but not all) Liberals recognised that this was no longer manageable. Increased government expenditure was unavoidable and therefore additional government income had to be raised. Moreover, if the Liberals failed to devise a financially effective and politically attractive strategy, then, willy-nilly, the Conservatives would push through tariff reform.

These were the immediate considerations lying behind Lloyd George's planning of the notorious People's Budget in 1909. However, its scope was ambitiously enlarged by the incorporation of other long-standing personal and political objectives. On the one hand, he wanted to accumulate additional revenue to pay for further welfare projects he had in mind, in particular, to assist the sick, unemployed, widows and orphans. Furthermore, building on his Board of Trade experience, he proposed in the budget to extend still more the economic role of the state by creating a Development Commission to stimulate in particular the revival of rural industry, for example with afforestation schemes. On the other hand, when it came to raising revenue, his instincts were principally to rely on direct taxation. Hence the budget imposed higher death duties, increased income taxes and included a supertax on the very rich. There were in addition highly controversial land taxes. The landed elite had long been the victims of Lloyd George's verbal abuse, and they were now vulnerable to his plans to raise revenue, for example by taxing on sale or transfer the unearned increase in the value of their land, which often followed from adjacent urban development or industrial enterprise, and by levying a duty on the capital value of the undeveloped land they kept locked up. Lloyd George's sympathies were directed to those who made productive use of resources, the entrepreneurs, rather than those he condemned as the wealthy parasites who fed off their achievements. Important for Lloyd George was the introduction of a land valuation system which he intended would provide the state with the data for later more far-reaching land reforms. Finally, there was some increase in indirect taxation: new petrol taxes and motor car licences (to pay for roads), which affected in those days only the very wealthy, higher duties on tobacco and, symptomatic of his antipathy to the drink trade, a sharp rise in the cost of liquor licences and new duties on spirits. There were precedents for some of these innovations in earlier Liberal budgets (death duties introduced in 1894, higher taxation on unearned income in 1907), but nothing so ambitious. What was radical and innovative about this budget was not simply the amount of money Lloyd George aimed to raise but the social reforms he intended the raising of the money as well as its expenditure to effect. It was an exercise in social engineering, taxing the rich principally for the benefit of the poor.

The speech, lasting four and a half hours, with which Lloyd George introduced this budget to the House of Commons on 29 April 1909 confirmed his commitment to the New Liberalism. Moreover, he demonstrated that raising vast amounts of new revenue was compatible with the maintenance of free trade. The howls which followed reflected not just the hostility of the rich and particularly of the landowners to new taxation, echoed by some even in the Liberal cabinet, but the rage of Conservatives at Lloyd George's proof of the irrelevance of tariff reform. In combination, this explains why the House of Lords, packed by Tory backwoodsmen rarely seen before upon its stately benches, took the unprecedented step on 30 November 1909 of vetoing the budget by 350 votes to 75. Traditionally, the Lords had not challenged money bills, but they argued, with some justification, that this budget aimed at more than revenue-raising. The Lords thus unleashed a constitutional crisis.

It is very unlikely that Lloyd George had intended his budget to be rejected. He had planned for his radical fund-raising to be followed by further constructive legislation so as to revive Liberal fortunes and to leave his mark. But once the Conservatives had begun to threaten the use of the veto he calculated that there might be additional political advantages to be reaped by widening the issue into a conflict between the Peers and the People. It was an interpretation which horrified the King and alarmed the dithering Asquith, but this was the message, for example, of his richly entertaining denunciation of their lordships in speeches at Limehouse in the East End of London in July 1909 and at Newcastle in October 1909 (where he referred contemptuously to the House of Lords as 'five hundred men, ordinary men chosen accidentally from among the unemployed' (quoted in John Grigg, *Lloyd George: The People's Champion 1902–1911*, 1978, p. 225).

A radical brought up in rural North Wales in the late nineteenth century was bound to identify the landed elite as the social enemy of progress. But it is evident that Lloyd George expected the campaign against the peers and for the termination of their veto to rally mass support nationally. This was not just a bid for the backing of those Nonconformist or Welsh interest groups whose programmes had suffered at the hands of the Lords and who looked to Lloyd George for rescue. Nor was it simply an attempt to improve his credentials among the working class, who perhaps stood to gain from state social reform. Lloyd George also wanted to encourage support for the Liberals among the professional and commercial middle classes whose meritocratic values and entrepreneurial zeal ought to be offended by inherited, unearned and therefore undeserved aristocratic privilege. Lloyd George was denounced for setting class against class: in fact he aimed to unite all those who earned their living, middle class and working class, against a privileged elite. This had, after all, been central to much traditional nineteenth-century radical thinking and in the past an electorally attractive feature of Liberalism. The question remained whether it retained its potency.

The first test came in January 1910 when a general election was fought on the issue of the budget versus tariff reform and, of course, over the powers of the Lords. Lloyd George was the principal figure around whom the battle raged. In Caernarfon Boroughs he triumphed with a majority of 1,078 votes, but elsewhere the Liberal victory was flawed and the dominance secured in 1906 was much reduced. Probably the Liberals did better than they would have done had an election been held in the doldrum months before the budget crisis erupted, but there were many losses, particularly in the rural and quasi-feudal south of England. With 275 MPs to the Conservatives 272, the Liberals had become dependent on the support of Labour with their 40 seats and on the Irish Nationalists with their 82. This last meant that the Home Rule issue could be ignored no longer.

Moreover, the election had only resolved the issue of the 1909 budget, which the Lords now grumpily let pass. Lloyd George was insistent that the victory of the People over the Peers be carried through to its legislative conclusion, but the process proved to be unexpectedly prolonged. Asquith had feebly accepted the King's demand that the Liberals should fight and win a second general election before he be obliged to create enough peers to force through the House of Lords a Parliament Bill which would abolish their absolute veto. Edward VII then inconveniently died on 6 May 1910, and party leaders felt obliged to see if the crisis facing the new king, George V, could not be solved by inter-party negotiation. The failure of these talks by November was followed by a second election in December 1910, resulting in an increased majority of 1,208 votes for Lloyd George in Caernarfon Boroughs but a still narrower government victory: Liberals and Conservatives both won 272 seats, making the Liberals still more dependent on their allies, Labour with 42 seats and the Irish with 84. The Parliament Act which the Lords eventually and reluctantly passed in August 1911 left their membership unchanged, reduced the maximum duration of each Parliament from seven to five years, tightly defined the money bills which the Lords were obliged to pass, and left them with the right to use a powerful suspensory veto of at least two years over all other legislation. Nevertheless, the supremacy of the House of Commons had been unequivocally demonstrated: no prime minister has henceforth been a member of the Lords, and the abolition of the absolute veto did make possible subsequent radical legislation. Lloyd George could take satisfaction from that achievement and pleasure from his now secure status as the people's champion.

Yet for all his prominence in this public controversy, he was frustrated by such an unexpectedly prolonged crisis. For one thing, and not for the first time, he felt uneasy with the pretence required by such party political conflict. He was impatient, for example, with the critical response of some of his own colleagues to the terms of the People's Budget, in particular those blinkered by traditional Gladstonian notions of public finance. On the other hand he identified kindred spirits among the Opposition whose constructive objectives he admired, however much he dissented from their proposed methods, and who, he recognised, were hampered by their own party dinosaurs. During the inter-party constitutional talks in 1910 Lloyd George therefore discreetly proposed the formation of a temporary Coalition government. The country faced an emergency, he claimed, which required unusual measures. While he instanced the opportunities for agreement over Empire matters and foreign and defence policy and hinted at some compromise even over tariffs, it must be stressed that he was mainly seeking all-party support for a programme of domestic social reform to tackle housing, health insurance, unemployment, education, the poor law, alcohol abuse and agriculture. This remarkable initiative briefly attracted some support in both parties but then was snuffed out by party political loyalties and genuine and irreconcilable differences of opinion, particularly over Ireland. It indicated Lloyd George's occasional political naivety – a wish for things to be other than they obviously were – rather than a lack of principle. He was not seeking personal power through this scheme, and he remained loyal to his primary reforming objectives. However, his political experience to date, in office and out, had persuaded him that, although the world was full of apparently conflicting interests, much of value could be accomplished by negotiation and compromise.

The collapse of this secret initiative obliged him to press on in the face of resumed party political conflict with his now maturing plans for further far-reaching social reforms. He had flagged his intentions when he had described old age pensions in 1908 as just the first of the Liberal government's welfare innovations, but the final proposals for health and unemployment insurance were not presented to Parliament until May 1911.

The delay reflected partly the distraction caused by political crises but also the complex private negotiations which seemed to precede all Lloyd George's major initiatives. Alarmed by the cost of non-contributory pensions, he had concluded that the scheme for compulsory state insurance he now planned must be contributory, drawing resources from employer and employee as well as the state. This was the basis of the few other state-run, though rather more restricted, schemes operating elsewhere in Europe which Lloyd George had taken time to investigate, beginning with a trip to Germany in 1908. He was also much influenced when devising health insurance by the friendly society tradition of private insurance popular among skilled workers at home and by the operations of the industrial insurance companies. Indeed, he was obliged to negotiate carefully and at length with these powerful vested interests who feared the intrusion of state competition. Ultimately he had to incorporate them into the running of his scheme as 'approved societies', and he was forced to sacrifice plans for widows' and orphans' pensions in order to buy their support. Trade unions too, suspicious of a compulsory and contributory scheme, had to be included and allowed to administer benefits, a concession which helped considerably their recruiting of new members. In addition Lloyd George had to exert all his charm and cunning to navigate around the obstacles thrown in his way by the medical profession, anxious to protect its professional integrity – and its income. Doctors were a rather more potent lobby than the bizarre coalition of duchesses and their maids who later led a campaign against compulsory insurance for domestic servants. All this explains why the National Insurance Act was not passed until December 1911 and why the scheme did not begin to distribute benefits until January 1913.

The Act's passage and implementation were formidable legislative and administrative achievements. Winston Churchill had taken over the preparation of Part II of the measure, which established unemployment insurance for some 2.25 million mainly skilled manual workers in trades vulnerable to cyclical depression. More complex was Part I, through which Lloyd George secured health insurance for all manual workers and others on modest incomes (below £160 a year), an estimated 10 million men and 4 million women. They were guaranteed sickness, disability and maternity benefits and free access to and treatment by a doctor, the majority for the first time in their lives. The two parts therefore reduced the risk that workers who lost their jobs or fell sick would be forced to depend on the hated Poor Law. By inserting a minimum state safety net, the Act was designed to maintain or to restore the health and therefore the efficiency of workers when afflicted by unemployment or sickness. This was not expected to discourage them from taking further personal measures to protect themselves and their families.

This achievement did not, however, obliterate the challenges facing either Lloyd George or the Liberal party. By-election losses in 1911–12 suggested that contributory national insurance was not going to be sensationally popular, at least not until its benefits had been experienced. Besides, Lloyd George was not the man to relax. He believed the programme of social reforms which the Liberals had launched remained incomplete, and he also aimed to tackle the complex issues of landownership and taxation which his 1909 budget had first addressed. In 1912 he therefore began to prepare yet another radical programme, his land campaign. The investigations he sponsored, greatly assisted by Seebohm Rowntree, were expected to lead to more legislative, administrative and taxation reforms, and these were intended to ease serious social difficulties, further enhance Lloyd George's reputation as a constructive radical, sustain the electoral appeal of New Liberalism and dish the Opposition. One inspiration was certainly his old radical hostility to landowners. But his anxieties about the decline of agriculture, the consequent impoverishment of rural society, the migration of population from countryside to town and the debilitating social consequences of low pay, unemployment and overcrowded slum housing were widely shared across the political parties and among many social commentators. The campaign therefore had considerable political potential, although the ap-propriate solutions to these social and economic problems were, of course, much disputed, even within the Liberal party.

Lloyd George's Land Enquiry Committee recommended state schemes to generate rural prosperity and to enhance rural living standards, such as minimum wages and better housing for agricul-tural workers, plus fair rents and security of tenure for farmers. In addition, there were to be public measures to improve urban conditions, especially by compulsory town planning, local rate reforms and state-assisted land purchase and housebuilding. The scale and range of the land campaign was therefore much more extensive (and urban) than its title might suggest. The rural proposals were matured first, and Lloyd George persuaded his colleagues to endorse their principles and to authorise his launch of a public information and propaganda campaign in October 1913. The urban campaign had barely begun and no legislation had been formulated in detail before the outbreak of war, but already there had been encouraging responses from many rural and some urban constituencies.

Further evidence of Lloyd George's still adventurous style can be seen in his related budget of 1914. Obliged yet again to raise exceptional amounts of revenue for naval armaments, he planned once more to increase direct taxation, introducing a graduated income tax on earned incomes and increasing supertaxes, death duties and taxes on unearned incomes. But he also aimed to use the budget once more for the purposes of social reform by proposing to recycle some of these assets as central government grants to local authorities for education, roads, policing and some health schemes including maternity clinics, thus compelling councils to improve services while allowing them to reduce local rates. He also announced the rating of site values. In parliamentary terms the budget was a disaster since its more radical proposals were judged by the Speaker to step beyond the terms of a money bill as defined by the Parliament Act and were therefore vulnerable to the veto of the House of Lords. There was even a rebellion among troubled Liberals. Compromises had to be made and site value rating and the local authority grants postponed. Although Lloyd George's reputation as a legislator suffered, his credentials as a financial radical survived. In consequence it is quite probable that Lloyd George would have faced with confidence the general election expected in 1915.

It is true that in these last pre-war years he had also taken some personal risks. In January 1913 Frances Stevenson, his daughter's former tutor and his current private secretary, became his mistress. Thanks to her discretion and Margaret's reluctant toleration, his public position did not suffer. Indeed, the new relationship introduced an unusual stability and domesticity into Lloyd George's personal life. However, his personal reputation in political circles never fully recovered from the accusations in 1912–13 that with others he had used his public position to profit from dealings in Marconi shares: technically innocent, he had been extremely foolish and less than frank in his self-defence. Lloyd George was not greedy for money, but he entered politics with comparatively modest financial resources and he desired the security which wealth would bring. As in his politics, he was certain in his aims but not over-scrupulous in his means.

Moreover, there remained for Lloyd George and for the Liberal party an outstanding agenda of politically dangerous business. Another Welsh Disestablishment Bill was finally introduced in April 1912 but its parliamentary passage was protracted until September 1914 by the Lords' use of their suspensory veto. The bill's introduction was greeted without enthusiasm by most observers in England, and the disendowment terms and the delayed passage irritated those in Wales who cared. Lloyd George carefully limited his personal involvement. Moreover, neither Lloyd George nor the Liberal party appeared to emerge with electoral credit from their compromise proposal in 1914 to solve the crisis over Irish

Home Rule by the exclusion of Ulster: civil war still seemed imminent. Furthermore, the Liberal party had not solved the question of votes for women. Lloyd George readily accepted the principle (even though militants dynamited his new house in 1913) and favoured a generous measure of adult suffrage which would include votes for working-class women. Anything less, he believed, would enfranchise mainly propertied women and therefore benefit the Conservatives. Asquith's hostility to women's suffrage (not eased by being horse-whipped by angry suffragettes), the Speaker's blocking of the most promising manoeuvre in 1913 and thereafter other priorities frustrated radical electoral reform. Nor could the Liberal government offer sufficient answers to the rash of industrial strikes between 1910 and 1914 which pushed to record heights the number of working days lost. At least Lloyd George enhanced his reputation by resolving in August 1911 a rail dispute which Asquith had mishandled, although he was less successful the following year during strikes of coal miners and dock workers.

Was the Liberal party and therefore also Lloyd George threatened before 1914 by a Labour movement perhaps willing and able to exploit these weaknesses? At parliamentary level the Labour party seems to have been held in check. In the Commons, they chose to act as loyal allies so as to keep the government in power, and though the general elections of 1910 had witnessed substantial Labour advances, thereafter in by-elections Labour at best enjoyed an increase in their share of the vote. A close scrutiny of local elections shows increasing grass roots support for Labour, but only in certain areas like Clydeside, South Wales, parts of London and West Yorkshire. However, the increasing numbers of trade unionists and especially of those affiliating to the Labour party could be interpreted as ominous for the future of Liberalism, particularly in the period of industrial unrest. Liberal ideals were attractive in a society which perceived a close community of interest between workers and employers; social and economic changes threatening to split society and induce class conflict spelt danger. Nevertheless, it remained highly unlikely in 1914 that the Labour party at least in the near future could thrive alone and would risk severing their progressive alliance with the Liberals.

The pre-eminence of the Liberal party in that partnership owed, of course, not a little to Lloyd George's activities. Moreover, he had also been greatly responsible for the simultaneous disarray of the Conservative party. During the late nineteenth century the

43

Conservatives had come to believe themselves the natural party of government, but beginning in 1906 they had gone through the harrowing experience of losing three successive general elections. Furthermore, their arrogant use of the privileges of the House of Lords had been ultimately counter-productive and its prerogatives had been permanently trimmed. They were also troubled by the prospects of further parliamentary reform, including votes for women. And they had allowed Lloyd George and other Liberals to set much of the political agenda, particularly in the area of social reform and public finance. Tariff reform had failed adequately to attract the country, whereas it had visibly split the party. Not surprisingly, the Conservatives exploited the issue of Ulster and Home Rule as their most potent weapon. And, characteristically, in 1911 they dumped their unsuccessful leader, Balfour, and set up the more abrasive Bonar Law.

Obviously it would be an exaggeration to ascribe all these Liberal advantages to Lloyd George, and we must not overlook the reforming and constructive contribution of such colleagues as Churchill, Herbert Gladstone and even Asquith. But at a general election in 1915 the Liberal manifesto would probably have proposed what Lloyd George was busy devising, programmes for urban renewal and rural recovery. The Liberals would also have reminded the electorate of their innovative use of the powers of the state and would have presented for approval their welfare legislation, their financial initiatives and the scalp of the House of Lords. In brief, the election would have been virtually a referendum on Lloyd George's achievements since 1906 and on his proposals for the future.

4
The man who won the war?
1914–18

Instead of a general election there was to be a world war. The Great War of 1914–18 has been described as a total war, the first large-scale conflict between modern industrialised nations and one which tested the full range of their resources: size, physical quality and morale of populations, industrial and agricultural productivity, external trade connections, financial assets and credit, institutional adaptability and social and political cohesion. Military skills might seem almost secondary. Furthermore, it has been argued that the severity and duration of the test inevitably exposed weaknesses, forced changes, checked pre-war activities, extended other unexpected opportunities and, in sum, precipitated developments evident in the post-war world. The testing and transforming effect of total war may also be discerned in the career of Lloyd George. Beginning the war as Chancellor of the Exchequer in a Liberal government, in May 1915 he became Minister of Munitions in a Coalition administration and in July 1916 Secretary of State for War. In December 1916, at the age of 53, he was appointed Prime Minister: without the war he may never have achieved such fame.

Nevertheless, there is a danger of exaggerating the impact of war upon him. It is not the case, for example, as some disillusioned post-war critics bitterly claimed, that Lloyd George was once a pacifist and anti-imperialist who simply abandoned his principles in August 1914. As already indicated, from his early days he had shown a regard for the status and interests of Great Britain and her Empire;

his opposition to the Boer War was a discriminating attack upon that particular act of imperial aggression. Moreover, his well-recorded objections as chancellor before the war to the huge increases in naval estimates demanded by pushy First Lords of the Admiralty, particularly McKenna in 1909 and 1911 and then Churchill in 1914, were based on the premise that the British naval supremacy that he was as determined as anyone to maintain would be secure even without such aggressive additions. Noticeably, on these occasions, though he might bluster and even threaten resignation, he found the money and remained in office. Furthermore, on his own initiative and with the approval of senior colleagues, he reacted to the German threat to France and the Entente in the Agadir crisis of 1911 with an unambiguous public warning to Germany.

It would, however, be going too far to regard Lloyd George before 1914 as a zealous advocate of a strong imperial and defence policy. As chancellor and a senior minister he was naturally familiar with, and had no objections to, the general principles which guided Grey's diplomacy and British rearmament, but his personal attention to foreign and imperial affairs was patchy. The record shows unequivocally that he had made domestic reforms his priority and it was for those that he wished mainly to accumulate government revenue. Indeed, his most consistent contribution to foreign affairs had been to try to encourage settlements with the Central Powers (for example, during his trip to Germany in 1908 and in his support for Haldane's mission in 1912) which would allow national resources to be devoted to the tools of peace rather than the weapons of war. Until August 1914 the land campaign and a forthcoming election to be fought on domestic issues were his priorities. Moreover, these preferences and his long-established credentials as a man of the left made him sensitive to the views of radicals and Nonconformists whose support had sustained much of his career to date; and until 1914 many of these tended towards isolationism, anti-militarism or liberal internationalism. To an extent, therefore, Lloyd George was inhibited in his response to external affairs, at least in public, by the views and expectations of his supporters.

His dilemma was painfully exposed in the crisis of July and August 1914. On the one hand he was conscious that some radicals and Nonconformists objected to actions likely to draw Great Britain into a continental war in defence of France and Tsarist Russia. Moreover, in spite of patriotic cheering crowds outside, he did not shed his old Baptist belief that war was evil. On the other hand, he was persuaded that Germany's actions were aggressive and unjustified, first in her support for Austria's attack on Serbia, second in her mobilisation against Russia with its implicit threat to France and finally in her violation of the neutrality of Belgium. This last act brought most of the waverers in the Liberal cabinet around to supporting British intervention. It is probable in Lloyd George's case that his decision was swayed less by the rights of small neutral nations than by his reluctant acceptance that only war could protect the English Channel and therefore the national security to which he had always been committed. He was not alone in assuming that the defence of apparent British interests constituted a just war.

Lloyd George's decision to support the ultimatum to Germany therefore marked a real if, in his view, unavoidable shift in his political priorities. Thereafter he never wavered in his conviction that the war would have to be fought through to a complete victory, and he dissented from later proposals for a compromise peace. Indeed, as the war progressed he was tempted by the prospect of British gains, for example in the Middle East at the expense of Turkey. He became a harder man: war brutalises its practitioners. His public reputation consequently began to change, to the dismay of some former admirers and the delighted surprise of some pre-war opponents. Moreover, Lloyd George was not among those who believed this would be a short sharp conflict, over by Christmas. He foresaw a long and strenuous struggle which would make sustained, profound and definitely novel demands upon the nation.

It is, however, continuity rather than change which is most striking in his own response to the demands of waging total war. It is ironic that the career of this distinguished peacetime minister had unwittingly developed in him the instincts and the administrative and political skills peculiarly appropriate for wartime. Indeed, the war gave Lloyd George extraordinary liberty to tackle government business in the manner to which he had been drawn before the war. The result was to be a transformation of the relationship between state and society, but along predictable lines.

Before the war on numerous occasions he had revealed his loose commitment to strict party political loyalties and his interest in cross-party co-operation. From August 1914 he was certain that the attention of all politicians should be focused exclusively on the waging of war. He therefore welcomed the party political truce agreed in the national emergency. As chancellor he formally consulted opposition leaders on the measures necessary to calm London's jittery financial markets. More dramatically, when the course of the war was going badly for the Allies he was instrumental in encouraging Asquith in May 1915 to turn the Liberal government into a Coalition by including leading Conservatives and even a representative of the labour party. Such a gesture, in Lloyd George's view, would not only enhance the political and adminis- trative talent at the centre but should eliminate distracting party political controversies. When the government was reconstructed in December 1916 and he became prime minister, its Coalition character was retained, out of personal preference as well as political necessity. Naturally, divisive pre-war issues ought to be evaded: the land campaign ceased with the outbreak of war and the Welsh Disestablishment and Home Rule Bills, though passed in September 1914, were promptly suspended for the duration with his approval.

As a minister before the war Lloyd George had become convinced that *laissez-faire* alone would not secure either Britain's economic efficiency or her social well-being. He therefore needed no con- vincing that the massive mobilisation needed in wartime could only be accomplished when directed by the state. War on the scale and for the duration he expected required the state to tap all available resources. These included financial assets, materials and manpower (more accurately 'personpower'); they might be located overseas but mainly lay at home; and allocating as well as raising these resources required central supervision. The demands of war (like those of peace) were too insistent to be left merely to exhortation, volunteering or the free market.

For example, he was convinced that the ability of the Allies, and not just of Great Britain, to wage war depended on British financial strength. Hence he acted swiftly and effectively in August 1914, publicly pretending that there would be 'business as usual' even while taking extraordinary steps to use the credit of the state to restore confidence to the fragile private sector. Thereafter, in his war budgets he increased government income by pushing up rates of taxation and especially by using the sustained creditworthiness of the government to raise war loans at home and abroad. He was not a great war financier, relying too much on loans and not enough on taxation, but he had at least demonstrated his early awareness of the scale, and therefore probable cost to government, of the war.

More radical and dramatic were his responses to the material demands of war. The proper supply of munitions was vital.

48

Traditionally this was the responsibility of the War Office, who relied on the state arsenals and a selected group of trusted private companies like Vickers Armstrong. Lloyd George was soon convinced that extended state action was essential. In the first place, the Russian forces depended upon a plentiful supply of arms from their more industrialised ally. In addition, the huge volunteer army which Kitchener had set about raising demanded a similarly massive expansion in the output of munitions: parading with wooden rifles was neither good training nor helpful for morale. Besides, with trenches on the Western front rapidly scarring the landscape between the Channel and Switzerland, the war of movement ceased and the demand rose for more machine guns, mortars, heavy artillery and endless supplies of ammunition. Ultimately, a munitions crisis helped bring about the formation of the Coalition government in May 1915 and, as a consequence, Lloyd George's appointment as the first Minister of Munitions. We should not ignore the War Office's own earlier achievements in increasing their orders, in recruiting some extra engineering firms and even in building the first new national shell factory – although we must note that much of this was due to the pressure which Lloyd George had exerted as a member of the cabinet committees set up at his suggestion to monitor supplies. Nor should we believe everything that he wrote subsequently in his memoirs about the success of the Ministry of Munitions under his direction, nor ignore the confusion of procedures which sometimes frustrated its administrators. Nevertheless, the statistics show that a huge increase in output was effected and important new weapons were put into production. Sixty more state munitions factories were built by the end of 1915 and many new private companies were recruited, all operating under tight central direction.

Lloyd George was also aware that government lacked the managers and the management skills to direct industrial production on the scale demanded by war. As a minister before the war he had become doubtful about the administrative vitality of many, though not all, civil servants but much impressed by the imagination and energy of entrepreneurs. In the crisis of war he therefore turned for help to men of 'push-and-go' as he described them. Unlike labour, they were not to be conscripted but persuaded. For example, the co-operation of managers of engineering firms was secured by the promise of large government contracts, capital for expansion, supplies of machine tools, the labour they needed and the promise of generous profit margins. More remarkably, Lloyd George also went 'head-hunting' and brought into the central administration of the Ministry of Munitions successful entrepreneurs and professional managers from the private sector. His ability to pick enough effective operators, like Eric Geddes from the North Eastern Railway Company, was one key to the success of the Ministry of Munitions.

On becoming prime minister Lloyd George was certain that further bureaucratic innovations were needed in order to squeeze out still more of the nation's resources to meet the needs of total war and to allocate such assets more effectively. Naturally, he was convinced that what he had earlier accomplished at Munitions could be achieved elsewhere, if the right people were put in charge. Several more government departments were created and more state controls imposed. For example, the production and distribution of foodstuffs had become crucial; German U-boats were beginning to devastate British shipping and the food imports upon which the British people were dangerously dependent. Lloyd George sponsored the Corn Production Act in 1917 which extended state supervision over farmers and increased output, and he appointed a Food Controller to tackle problems of distribution. True, the duties of this office clashed untidily with those of the Board of Agriculture and the Board of Trade, and Lord Devonport, one of those entrepreneurial men-of-push-and-go, proved a hopeless appointment. But Lord Rhondda, his successor, another businessman, was a more shrewd selection who resolved the key problems of food prices and supply by introducing financial subsidies in 1917 and rationing in 1918. Lloyd George tackled an associated problem by appointing Sir Joseph Maclay, a shipping company owner, to the new post of Shipping Controller: under his direction the construction of the merchant ships needed to replace those sunk by U-boats was speeded up and shipping was more efficiently used.

Lloyd George also had to confront the critical question of manpower. His pre-war experience had made him more know-ledgeable than most ministers of the importance to industry and agriculture of adequate and reliable labour supplies, and his involvement in industrial disputes had given him valuable experience in negotiating with trade unions. Increasing the output of munitions and other goods essential in war required more labour in those key areas. That could only be arranged, he knew, with the consent of trade unions who, mainly representing skilled workers, were concerned to preserve their hard-won status and rewards. He succeeded in persuading their representatives in March 1915 to accept the so-called Treasury Agreement by which for the duration of the war the unions agreed to outlaw strikes and to allow dilution, letting unskilled labour take over some of the tasks previously reserved under restrictive practices to the skilled. However, legislation was subsequently passed to make this compulsory in the munitions industry. Among the many new workers brought into vital industries between July 1915 and the end of the war were a further 1.25 million women, thus effecting, if only for the duration, a remarkable social as well as economic transformation.

This was still not enough. Recruiting huge volunteer armies was actually damaging the war effort by encouraging precious skilled workers to depart for France when their most valuable contribution to the war effort could be made at home in industry. Trying to persuade the War Office to be more selective about the volunteers they accepted was only a partial cure. Accordingly, Lloyd George concluded that labour would be efficiently employed only within a state-managed system which would keep essential workers in key jobs while conscripting many of the rest into the armed services. Others, mainly Conservatives, agreed, and their insistence, plus the insatiable appetite of the Western front, forced Asquith's government to introduce such an unprecedented scheme during 1916. But manpower remained a perplexing domestic issue, which Lloyd George even as prime minister never properly resolved. Supply was limited, indeed diminishing as casualties grew, and the needs of army and of industry still competed. His own administration included not only a new Ministry of Labour but a rival Ministry of National Service. The latter was supposed to encourage greater mobility of industrial workers for war purposes and perhaps to weed out labour inappropriately preserved in reserved occupations. The resulting confusion made a lifelong enemy for Lloyd George out of its frustrated first minister, the Lord Mayor of Birmingham, Neville Chamberlain. His successor, Auckland Geddes, another business manager, was given more specific powers and proved more effective in protecting the manpower needs of the home front albeit at the expense of the military. Extending conscription early in 1918 to a wider age range indicated how desperate Lloyd George found the manpower equation.

An indication of the continuity of Lloyd George's former concerns into the war years is that he did not ignore such opportunities as cropped up to advance democratic and social reforms. For example, following the introduction of so many more women into the munitions industry he authorised Rowntree in 1915 to set about the improvement of factory welfare conditions. Later, as prime minister, he encouraged the formation of joint councils of employers and employees to try to resolve disputes over pay and conditions without strike action. In an inspired move he appointed to his government the historian H.A.L. Fisher to plan the expansion of education after the war, and he transformed the Reconstruction Committee set up by Asquith into a proper Ministry, charged with preparing programmes of post-war economic development and social reforms. Similarly, he accepted the conclusions of an inter-party conference which had reviewed the electoral system, and endorsed the most radical of all parliamentary reforms in 1918, granting the franchise to virtually all adult males and, at last, most women over the age of 30. Undoubtedly, as always with Lloyd George, such social and political innovations concealed mixed motives. Genuinely he hoped that some would ease the burdens of the people. But he also intended such gestures to maintain public commitment to the war effort and political support for his administration.

The success of mobilisation compared with the frustration of the military campaigns had convinced Lloyd George by 1916 that his methods were also essential at the centre of government. He complained correctly about the lack of directing authority from Asquith at the top. He was also certain that most members of the cabinet lacked the time and the expertise to decide collectively on major strategies for the home and fighting fronts; he therefore urged that this should be made the responsibility of a small new cabinet committee with proper executive powers. It should include Lloyd George but normally exclude Asquith, leaving him free for other prime ministerial duties. This plan won the support of Bonar Law, and for a while it even gained the grudging consent of Asquith. But on 4 December the prime minister changed his mind and dismissed the proposal. Lloyd George, in despair, thereupon resigned. But Asquith now found that he had jeopardised the support of too many colleagues in the Coalition, especially among the Conservatives, to carry on his administration. He also rejected a compromise, for not wholly admirable personal reasons, which would have allowed him to retain office in a government containing Lloyd George but led by either Bonar Law or Balfour. The Conservative leaders thereupon turned to Lloyd George as the only man seemingly capable of commanding the support of enough Liberals and Conservatives in the House of Commons, and of organised labour in the country, to form a new Coalition government. It would be naive to claim that Lloyd George had never aspired to becoming prime minister, but historians no longer seriously believe that he had conspired to bring Asquith down. Rather, in his determination to strengthen the executive centre of the state in the emergency of war, he had precipitated a crisis whose final resolution on 7 December 1916 unexpectedly saddled him with the office of prime minister and the duty to put right that which he believed was wrong.

Responsibility for running the war was henceforth concentrated in the hands not of the cabinet as a whole, nor of a small cabinet committee such as he had proposed to Asquith, but of a select war cabinet which Lloyd George chaired but which included just a handful of other senior men largely freed from departmental duties: initially Bonar Law and Curzon, both Conservatives, Milner, notionally a Conservative but with independent views, and Henderson from the Labour party. Lloyd George was the only Liberal. Other ministers and advisers were summoned to its deliberations as required. It has been argued that the war cabinet never quite lived up to expectations: in spite of almost daily meetings it was swamped by the tremendous volume of work generated by a world war, some business had to be devolved to committees, and too often it found itself merely arbitrating between disputing departments. Nevertheless, the suitability of a war cabinet for top level policy-making in wartime is suggested by its revival during the Second World War (and in later conflicts).

Lloyd George was responsible for another belated and lasting addition to government bureaucracy, the cabinet secretariat. In the past, cabinets had met without any formal system for the presentation of papers, the recording of decisions and the issuing of instructions to departments. Lloyd George developed an efficient secretariat which helped improve the qualities of government decision-making and the execution of decisions. He also created his own prime ministerial secretariat, lodged in huts at the bottom of the garden at 10 Downing Street and hence known as the 'Garden Suburb'. He needed a larger personal staff, in addition to his private secretaries (including Frances Stevenson), to support his enormous range of activities, and he also valued such an independent source of information and advice. The prime minister's office has since become another regular feature of modern government.

Mobilisation and bureaucratic innovations were all, of course, primarily intended to help the generals win the war, and their repeated failures made him bitter. It is tempting to interpret the tension between Lloyd George and the Army's High Command as a continuation of his pre-war hostility towards the landed elite from whom so many army leaders were socially drawn. His antagonism was also compounded by their resistance to civilian control over their operations, which Lloyd George (and Asquith) insisted was proper in a democracy. But above all, he had grounds for scepticism about their professional expertise as the casualties piled up to no avail at Ypres, Loos, the Somme, etc. However, becoming prime minister did not make Lloyd George the master over military strategy. For all his apparent authority he could not ignore the extraordinary (and misplaced) public confidence in the likes of Field-Marshal Haig and Admiral Jellicoe, expressed particularly in the press and by Conservatives. It took a long time before Jellicoe could be persuaded in 1917 to experiment with the technique of convoys which proved to be the best answer to the U-boat challenge. Lloyd George also found it difficult, perhaps because it was not possible, to present plausible alternatives to the apparently authoritative strategic appraisals presented by the professionals, although their lack of imagination filled him with despair. In war, as in peace, Lloyd George looked for devious solutions once frontal assault looked unavailing, but he was unable to convince the military or even all his colleagues that campaigns in the Balkans, on the Italian front and in Palestine were more capable of bringing victory than attrition on the Western front, and he never developed the political strength and perhaps the self-confidence to insist. Obliged to tolerate Haig's brutal attack in the summer of 1917 which sank in the swamp of Passchendaele, Lloyd George resorted thereafter to denying him the manpower for more slaughter and contrived to subordinate him to the Supreme War Council set up in November 1917. But only when the German armies nearly broke through in March 1918 did Lloyd George finally end Haig's autonomy by putting British troops under the command of Marshal Foch.

It may be seen therefore that much was unchanged after Lloyd George became prime minister. His additions to government bureaucracy indicate his continuing faith, sometimes misplaced, in the managerial skills of entrepreneurs and in the virtues of state enterprise and control as the means of mobilising national resources for war. The new style cabinet and his secretariats improved the quality of decision-making but failed to eliminate all bottlenecks and conflicts. But most seriously neither his enhanced authority nor his extraordinary energy nor his fertile imagination enabled him to dictate to the High Command any rapid war-winning new strategy. Victory came only when the arrival of substantial numbers of fresh American troops coincided with Germany's military and domestic exhaustion.

Obviously, by its very nature, success for the Allies in this total war owed most to the efforts and sacrifices, willing and unwilling, of millions of men and women. This was a war by democracy if not intentionally for democracy. We should also not ignore the major initiatives first taken by Asquith's government (although many had been made on Lloyd George's insistence) or the managerial and inspirational contributions of others (although many were Lloyd George appointees). Nor should we overlook the waste and inefficiencies that remained even after Lloyd George became prime minister. Yet his contribution to the Allied and particularly the British war effort was enormous. He recognised earlier than many how this war would have to be fought, and he above all had the instincts, the experience and the confidence to mobilise resources and direct operations, at least on the home front, in the necessary way. It remains legitimate to regard Lloyd George as 'The Man Who Won the War'. Whether the price was worth paying is an ethical not a historical question.

5
Prisoner of the Tories,
1918–22

When the Armistice was announced on 11 November 1918 Lloyd George's eminence as the triumphant prime minister appeared secure. Yet on 19 October 1922 he was forced to resign, and four days later he left 10 Downing Street for the last time, his person as well as his government widely condemned. Only recently have attempts been made to present balanced accounts of the achievements of his last period in government and to offer non-partisan explanations of his fall. We need first to check the reliability of the political foundations upon which his post-war administration was built before assessing its record and the reasons for its collapse.

In the summer of 1918 Lloyd George began to contemplate his long-term political future. He had already decided to call a general election to strengthen his wartime dominance of the House of Commons when the sudden collapse of the German army in the autumn forced him to finalise his post-war strategy. 'The Man Who Won the War' could not look forward with unclouded cheerfulness to the approach of peace. He knew that he had become prime minister in 1916 only in response to a wartime emergency whose passing might eliminate the support he had been granted. Moreover, the way he had obtained power and the prolonged and painful character of the war thereafter had made the man formally responsible for the British experience particularly liable to criticism. Many of the actions he had felt obliged to take had threatened his standing among pre-war supporters without cementing the allegiance of new political allies. Though prime minister, he was vulnerable. Most dangerously, he had become a politician without a party.

One possibility was to mark the return of peace by the resignation of his government, the dissolution of the Coalition and the reunification of the Liberal party in time for the election. Such a programme had its attractions. Many rank and file Liberals yearned for unity, and Lloyd George might have expected in such company much support for the post-war international settlement and domestic reconstruction policies he had in mind. In retrospect it would have been for Lloyd George probably, and for Liberalism certainly, the wisest course.

But the hostility which he had generated among his notional fellow party members made this an unlikely scenario. Some radicals and Nonconformists still resented his part in the decision to go to war in August 1914; a few had deserted to the pacifist wing of the Labour party. Many more Liberals had been troubled by his unqualified commitment to achieving total victory and to the decidedly un-Gladstonian methods he had embraced. Conscription and state mobilisation were difficult to reconcile with Liberal views of civil liberties. At an Imperial War Conference held in 1917 Lloyd George had even accepted the possibility of tariffs and imperial preferences after the war. Moreover, many MPs and not just Liberals had found (and would continue to find) distasteful and unconstitutional his presidential style of government: his war cabinet, his personal secretariat, his rare appearances in the Commons whose business he left Bonar Law largely to run, his appointment of a minister like Maclay who even disdained to become an MP. There was also suspicion of the imperialist ideals of colleagues like Milner and some members of his 'Garden Suburb', though their influence was (and still is) exaggerated. And most importantly, of course, many Liberals in and out of Parliament never forgave him for his apparent disloyalty to Asquith. When Lloyd George became prime minister it was calculated that 85 out of 260 Liberal MPs refused to support his administration, and in May 1918 when Asquith forced a crucial division in the House of Commons (the Maurice debate) 98 Liberals voted against the government, only 71 in favour.

And who would lead the reunited Liberals? Asquith remained the formal leader of the Liberal party and controlled its organisation and assets, but it was inconceivable that Lloyd George would resign as prime minister and serve under him: Lloyd George's self-esteem, never small, had been further inflated by the adulation of the crowd. Moreover, when he offered Asquith prestigious office in his government in November 1918, he was neither surprised nor displeased when the old man nursed his grievances and turned him down. Besides, Lloyd George had no faith in the capacity of many of those Liberals outside his current supporters to tackle the political problems he expected to confront. The rift in the party looked permanent. For a while he even contemplated contesting the next election with his own separate Liberal party, planning to stitch up subsequently a parliamentary majority through alliances with other parties.

Ultimately, it was more attractive to secure such an alliance before the election by maintaining the apparently winning team, his Coalition. He believed that the cross-party administration he had favoured before as well as during the war was best suited, under his direction, to handle post-war domestic and international problems, with the minimum amount of distracting party political controversy. Moreover, this was a strategy favoured by most Conservative leaders, especially Bonar Law. Curiously, the Conservatives were nervous about their future in 1918: they had not won a general election since 1900 and were unsure how the newly created mass electorate (including women) would behave. Those Conservatives who had worked closely with Lloyd George had come to respect his qualities and they believed his charismatic leadership offered the best defence against the much feared growth of socialism. Of course, in addition, Bonar Law and his colleagues welcomed a proposition which perpetuated the split in the Liberal party. Coalition, then, made sense.

However, that did not mean that Conservatives had shed all their long-cherished suspicions of Lloyd George. They had been easily angered during the war, for example by his reappointment to office of Churchill and by his criticisms of military idols like Haig. Moreover, his attempts to resolve the Irish conflict after the Easter Rising and again at a National Convention he summoned in 1917–18 had rekindled pre-war hostilities. (The failure of these moves, incidentally, also alienated irrevocably the Irish Nationalists.) Similarly, his crusade to improve labour productivity by state control over the drink trade had aroused predictable wrath, and Conservatives correctly saw him smuggling in one of his pre-war land reform proposals when minimum wages for agricultural workers were incorporated in the Corn Production Act. In brief, living with Lloyd George would be a marriage of convenience, not true love.

Initially, Lloyd George would have preferred to retain also the co-operation of Labour. Before the war he had endeavoured to retain working-class political support for the Liberal party and for himself within a progressive movement which contained Labour as a junior partner. Moreover, during the war he had acknowledged that mobilisation depended upon the co-operation of trade unions, and he was certain that the problems of post-war reconstruction would be eased by continued consultation with their leaders.

Therefore for both long- and short-term reasons Lloyd George had become worried by popular unrest and left-wing political extremism in 1917 and 1918, in spite of his formal agreements with trade unions, the promotion of Labour men to high office and his promises of further social reform. There were many unofficial strikes, protests against rent and price rises, murmurs against military conscription and fears of industrial compulsion. Labour expectations were rising, fuelled by full employment, improvements in real wage levels and socialist rhetoric, especially after the Russian Revolution. Trade unions had increased their membership from 4.1 million to 6.5 million between 1914 and 1918. Moreover, the resignation of Henderson in August 1917 led to the reunification of the Labour party (split by the entry into the war), the drafting of a new constitution and programme and the building up of constituency organisations. Most importantly, Labour decided to leave the Coalition and to fight the next election not in tandem with the Liberals but, in truth, as their principal rivals for the allegiance of the left. This decision and Lloyd George's reaction ended the former progressive alliance. Thereafter Lloyd George exploited the threat of socialism and industrial militancy to justify the perpetuation of the Coalition as the bulwark against Bolshevism and the guarantor of good government and social stability.

He still claimed that his government would occupy the centre ground of British politics. It would at least exclude Tory diehards incapable of contemplating further extensions of state social reform and economic reconstruction, or unwilling to accept the kind of negotiated compromises he knew were necessary to resolve the problems of Ireland and of India, or too rampant in their commitment to tariff reform. On the other hand, he hoped to be equally free of Liberal ideologues, dumbly defensive of free trade, blindly committed to the ideals of the League of Nations at the expense of national self-interest and deaf to the need for tough action against political extremism at home. The positive content of his position was offered in his first election speeches and in the Coalition manifesto. Strikingly, he went out of his way to try to revive his credentials as a domestic reformer, promising to 'make Britain a fit country for heroes to live in'. In particular, he offered better housing for the working class and rural resettlement, echoes of the land campaign. While there might be some tariff protection for British industry against unfair competition, there would be no extra duties on food imports. The Irish question would be solved at last by a generous measure of Home Rule, excluding Ulster, and India would gradually be granted responsible government. Less emphasis was otherwise placed initially upon overseas affairs beyond a commitment to secure a just and lasting settlement at the forthcoming peace conference.

At the same time he set out to engineer the return to the Commons of Liberals loyal to himself and this Coalition programme. He needed their presence to balance his ostensible Conservative allies and to ensure adequate backing for those measures more likely to appeal to reforming Liberals than to conserving Tories. Bonar Law and the Conservative party managers agreed not to oppose about 150 Liberals, chosen somewhat erratically from those who had generally supported Lloyd George in the past, and these together with approved Conservative candidates were given what excluded Liberals described in disgust as the 'coupon', an official letter of support from both party leaders.

These pre-election manoeuvres came unstuck. Lloyd George partly misjudged the electorate of December 1918. The war had not sweetened the temper of the British people. Far from wanting to hear him promise social reform, some voters, whipped on by the popular press, wanted revenge, to hang the Kaiser, to expel aliens and to make Germany pay for the war by savage punitive reparation payments to the victors. Too many politicians joined in that ignorant and short-sighted cry. Eric Geddes promised to squeeze Germany 'until the pips squeak'. Lloyd George, who had resisted the mob during the Boer War and who in truth could afford politically to urge restraint, capitulated to passion. His denunciation of Germany degraded his promises of reform. After the election he was to find the expectations and passions he had supinely endorsed impossible to calm.

Moreover, even the electoral consequences were only super-ficially satisfactory. The Coalition could muster support from at least 526 MPs out of a House of Commons of 707; Lloyd George's leadership appeared to be triumphantly endorsed. But the reduction of the independent Liberals to a rump of 28 MPs (Asquith and other senior Liberals lost their seats) elevated the Labour party in spite of its mere 63 seats (but 2.4 million votes) to the role of principal opposition party and gave it unintended credibility. Moreover, Lloyd George's contingent of 133 Coalition Liberals was monstrously outweighed by the 383 Conservatives and Irish Unionists. Conservatives alone could muster a majority in the Commons (helped by the refusal of all 73 Sinn Fein members to take their seats). Later they would wonder whether they might have won the election as an independent party. Henceforth, Lloyd George governed on sufferance, the prisoner of the Tories.

His apparent personal popularity in 1918 and the imbalance between his ostensible Liberal and Conservative support eventually persuaded him that his political future lay in a decisive break from the party structures of the past. Most strikingly, in March 1920 he attempted to fuse together his Coalition Liberals and the bulk of the Conservatives. The historic Liberal party would be marginalised if not entirely extinguished, the diehard Tories would be jettisoned and a new consolidated party would concentrate on checking the rise of socialism at home, by judicious social and political reform, and on the wise defence of British interests overseas. Many Conservative leaders, especially those most perturbed by social unrest and the strength of post-war socialism, were dazzled by this vision. However, his Coalition Liberal ministers, whom Lloyd George had rather taken for granted, rejected fusion. They retained more loyalty than him to their Liberal inheritance, more suspicion of their Conservative colleagues and more reverence for the prospect of an eventual Liberal union. For once, his political manoeuverings flopped.

What remained was politically unstable. Asquith had been res-tored to the House of Commons and to the leadership of the independent Liberals at a by-election in February 1920. Several Coalition Liberals, subsequently disillusioned with Lloyd George, drifted over to his side. The others struggled to set up their own party organisation, but constituency roots were shallow. The feeble National Liberal party, distinct from Asquith's, was finally launched to no acclaim in January 1922. Lloyd George did little to help them, although he thereby perpetuated his own lack of party political support. At the same time, his continuing dependence upon the Conservatives was also cruelly exposed. In January 1922 he tried to persuade these partners to hold a general election, but the proposal was effectively vetoed as not in the interests of the Conservative party. He was thus denied a prime minister's most potent weapon, the authority to call an election at the time of his own choosing. Lloyd George had never much respected party politics, but his attempt to escape their conventions had left him dangerously exposed.

His survival therefore depended solely upon his government's achievements. Success alone would bring security. There were grounds for optimism. He had assembled a talented team, arguably more administratively and politically skilled than any other which graced British politics between the wars. The cabinet initially included all the senior Conservatives like Bonar Law, Balfour, Austen Chamberlain and F.E. Smith: most would remain remarkably loyal to the prime minister. There were also seven Liberals, a disproportionate number, indicative of Lloyd George's genuine attempt to establish a reforming government.

Any post-war administration would have faced daunting domestic difficulties. Demobilisation, the government's war debts and the restoration of the peacetime economy were urgent problems, and these priorities complicated efforts to introduce the social reforms which Lloyd George had promised. He left these duties mainly to his Liberal ministers, although he authorised their missions. They did not fail him. Addison at the newly created Ministry of Health pioneered a Housing Act in 1919 which fulfilled many of Lloyd George's pre-war aspirations: he launched a programme of council house building in Britain which most subsequent governments until recently broadly sustained. Fisher at the Board of Education used the authority of the 1918 Education Act to plan the raising of the school leaving age, a programme of school building and an improvement in teachers' pay, thus addressing another of Lloyd George's early radical goals. At the Board of Agriculture, Prothero followed more of Lloyd George's leads, promoting land settlement and aid for agriculture. Meanwhile the Ministry of Labour made unemployment insurance virtually universal for manual workers in 1920 and incorporated dependants' allowances in 1921. Motives as always were mixed, and some reforms were expected in part to defuse the perceived militancy of labour and to head off more radical socialist demands. Such measures, however much they owed in detail to ministerial initiatives, nevertheless supported for a while Lloyd George's claims still to be a radical reformer.

Unfortunately such commitments were difficult to sustain. By 1921 severe economic depression dominated the domestic political agenda. To their credit Lloyd George and some of his colleagues responded with schemes for unemployment relief works and financial aid for exporters, in keeping with his pre-war and wartime faith in state action to ease social distress. However, cuts in public expenditure, the most orthodox of strategies, were demanded by the Treasury, city financiers, the Federation of British Industries, most backbenchers (Liberal and Conservative) and most of the press. During 1921 council house building stopped, the expansion of education was halted, expensive agricultural reforms were reversed. Only expenditure on unemployment insurance, the dole, was driven inexorably upwards. Lloyd George's capitulation exposed the shallowness of his political support. Some of his Liberal colleagues despaired, Addison was driven to resign. And Labour emphasised to the electorate that Lloyd George had broken his promises.

By that time Lloyd George's already strained relationship with organised labour had been ruptured by his government's response to industrial unrest. After the war, many unionists had demanded not only a restoration of those pre-war industrial practices which dilution agreements had suspended but the consolidation if not further extension of those gains in pay and working conditions which the full employment of the war years had brought at last to so many. Strikes were called to back such claims. At the same time, Lloyd George was being driven by businessmen, thick along the Conservative backbenches, to restore another characteristic of pre-war industrial practices, namely private enterprise, and he was sensitive to their demands. Government economic controls were relaxed, and the wartime nationalisations of the railways and of the coal mines looked ripe for reversal. A Royal Commission under Lord Sankey had been set up in February 1919 to examine the coal industry, and the miners felt particularly betrayed when Lloyd George used its division of opinion as an excuse to return the mines to private hands. When the depression struck, employers responded by wage cuts to reduce costs, triggering off further defensive strike action. Working days lost exceeded even the pre-war peak, nearly

63

86 million in 1921. Lloyd George attempted as in the past to negotiate settlements, but his lack of sympathy for trade-union aspirations was revealed, and it was not unjust that workers heaped blame upon him. By 1922 he had weathered the worst, but defeated and frustrated unionists were going to be unforgiving. Even some Liberals and Conservatives blamed him for intensifying industrial and class conflict. His electoral popularity and that of the Coalition sank.

Lloyd George's limited success on the domestic front was probably partially caused by the far greater attention which he gave to external affairs. This priority was certainly justified by the urgency of such business, but he had also come to prefer during the war the role of international statesman, elevated above domestic party strife. He attended over twenty post-war international con- ferences as prime minister, in addition to the prolonged sessions at Paris which produced the Treaty of Versailles. As on the domestic front, his government's positive record never sufficiently compensated in the public eye for its negative content, and ulti- mately foreign affairs unsettled irrevocably his political authority at home.

It is clear for instance that he secured in the peace treaties which formally concluded the war much of what he wanted and most ministers, MPs and the press expected. Germany's naval challenge was removed, her army neutered, her European territory trimmed and her overseas empire dismembered. He also skilfully if unscrupulously evaded any binding commitment to defend France. But on the other hand he failed to satisfy public expectations of immediate and massive reparations payments and he did not bring the Kaiser to trial. He was also himself aware that some of the terms which he had been obliged to force upon the Germans, especially those respecting Germany's frontiers, could not form the basis of a lasting peace. Much of his subsequent diplomatic effort was therefore devoted with incomplete success to reconciling France and Germany and to resolving the reparations problem, upon terms which would not also offend political forces in Britain.

Complicating these tasks was the problem of Russia. Here too he endeavoured to be a realist. During 1919 he checked Churchill's irresponsible efforts to sweep the Bolsheviks out of Russia, settled for the protection of Eastern Europe against Bolshevik expansion and even insisted upon a trade treaty with the new regime in March 1921. Unfortunately, his government's attempt to arm the Poles against the Red Army in the summer of 1920 angered British labour, while many Conservatives regarded the trade treaty as short-sighted and immoral. Finally, his efforts to sponsor reconciliation in Europe seemed in ruins when the two outcasts, Germany and Russia, struck their own private deal at Rapallo in April 1922.

Even one of his major achievements was condemned by some people as an incomplete settlement or as having bought peace at too high a price. He had accepted before the war that Home Rule for Ireland must be granted, although excluding Ulster. Neither then nor during the war had anyone been able either to negotiate or to impose a settlement upon political forces already willing to kill for their cause. Confronted with the electoral victory of Sinn Fein in most of the country and massive civil disobedience, Lloyd George had at first authorised a policy of repression. This was carried out with singular (though they claimed justified) ferocity by the ex-servicemen recruited into the notorious 'Black and Tans' and 'Auxiliaries', thus demonstrating the brutalising effect of the Great War upon troops as well as upon their political leaders. But Lloyd George finally chose negotiation, and by a mixture of threat and sweet-talking secured in December 1921 the treaty which set up the Irish Free State. It was a settlement which brought peace at a price for half a century, but without enhancing Lloyd George's own personal authority in Britain. His reputation never recovered either with those who had been horrified by the previous use of force or with those Unionist irreconcilables who believed their version of Ireland had been betrayed.

The accumulating loss of trust in his leadership proved fatal when during 1922 Lloyd George appeared to be taking the country into an unnecessary war against Turkey. His policy derived from his wartime aim to build up Britain's authority in the Middle East, but sadly he allowed his judgement to be clouded by a legacy from his Nonconformist past, a prejudice against 'the unspeakable Turks' generated by Gladstone's famous crusade over Bulgaria almost half a century earlier. His belligerent support for an expanded Greek state against a Turkey already stripped of her Middle Eastern empire was disavowed during the Chanak crisis in September 1922 by France, by the dominions, by many backbenchers and even by some of his own junior ministers.

By this time too Lloyd George's personal reputation had taken a further dive. All prime ministers, then as now, nominate individuals for honours in return for political support or financial contributions to party coffers, and there was more than a touch of hypocrisy in the objections to Lloyd George's use of this patronage. However, as a Welsh outsider, untroubled by respect for the aristocracy, Lloyd George had encouraged a larger traffic in these baubles, particularly after the war. Lacking any other substantial financial resources, he traded on the vanity of the rich to build up a tidy little fund (some £3 million by 1922) for his own political use. Knighthoods were flogged off for around £10,000, a hereditary peerage for at least £50,000. The manner of these sales, the disreputable character of some of the 'worthies' honoured and Lloyd George's private management of the funds he accumulated troubled many Liberals and convinced Conservatives like Baldwin that Lloyd George was corrupting British political life.

All governments, especially those launched with huge initial majorities, expect to lose subsequent by-elections, but without fearing large-scale party rebellion. Lloyd George, however, was peculiarly vulnerable when Labour and independent Liberals (and even an independent Conservative) began to notch up successes against the Coalition. Lacking his own adequate party base and the means personally to enforce party discipline upon the Coalition's mainly Conservative rank and file, he was dependent on retaining their admiration or at least toleration. For a while the international as well as the domestic record of his government sufficiently attracted their support. But during 1922 murmurings in the party and among junior ministers began seriously to grow. There was increasing distaste for Lloyd George's presidential style of government and still more for his sale of honours. The reversal of much of the Coalition's domestic policy and its struggles with the depression had also damaged the government's credibility. And foreign and Irish affairs, for which Lloyd George had taken personal responsibility, had generated particular disquiet, or worse, and had culminated in the Chanak crisis. By the autumn many Conservative backbenchers, often urged on by party workers in the constituencies, believed that the Conservatives would be more successful if they were to face the electorate independently and on their own programme. They did not rule out the possibility of a future coalition with Liberals against the much feared Labour party, but they no longer believed that Lloyd George should be the inevitable leader of such a grouping or that he would be an electoral asset on their side.

However, before rank and file grumbles could be turned into rebellion a credible alternative leader was needed. At a meeting of the Conservative parliamentary party held at the Carlton Club on 19 October 1922 one was found. Bonar Law had retired from the government through ill-health in March 1921; out of office he had come to share the spreading disillusionment with Lloyd George's rule. At the meeting his authoritative presence and his critical speech emboldened the dissidents. Austen Chamberlain, the official leader of the Conservative party, remained stubbornly loyal to the prime minister and the Coalition as the best defence against the menace of socialism, but his inept attempt to squash dissent drove members to vote by 187 to 87 in favour of contesting the next election as an independent party. Lloyd George knew at once that he had forfeited too much Conservative support and that his depleted Liberal ranks were inadequate to sustain him. He promptly resigned. His fall, before not after a general election, makes plain what he was reluctant to accept, the importance of party in British politics.

6
Left outside,
1922–45

At the end of 1922 Lloyd George was only 59 years old, understandably tired after 17 years continuously in government, in need of a holiday (which he took in Spain, at first with Frances and then with Margaret), but still physically strong. Most observers expected, or feared, his return to high office. No one, least of all Lloyd George, imagined that henceforth he was fated to remain 'the goat in the wilderness'. It is tempting to pass rapidly over this last phase of his career as a disappointing anti-climax. But since his exclusion from power is intimately connected with the fate of the Liberal party, his activities after October 1922 have an importance beyond the biographical.

Lloyd George's fall from power and the manner of his going did not immediately clarify his political future. He had been so central to British politics for so long that most players could not initially imagine him losing the power to shift around the pieces to his own convenience. Men like Baldwin and MacDonald were obsessively fearful of what new schemes he might be plotting. Even the lack of a large loyal political party, which had been the cause of his downfall, left him apparently with the freedom to choose between a range of political options. In fact he was soon to discover how limited and unattractive was the choice.

Initially, he suspected that a renewed coalition with the Conservatives was likely. Many senior Conservatives, including Austen Chamberlain, Balfour and Lord Birkenhead (formerly F.E. Smith), remained loyal to him and had refused to join the government which Bonar Law had strung together out of former junior ministers and 'new boys', contemptuously referred to as the 'Second XI'. Its apparent mediocrity was expected shortly to lead to cries for help and the reselection of the old hands, including Lloyd George. Moreover, in those constituencies where Conservative MPs and party agents were most frightened by the advance of socialism the attraction of a resumed coalition with Lloyd George and his Liberals remained strong. To help along this possibility, Lloyd George cautiously refrained from attacking Bonar Law too vigorously during the general election he called in November 1922. Lloyd George did not believe that the Conservative party alone would win a majority of seats, and a hung parliament would open up interesting possibilities. In fact, the Conservatives secured a clear majority with 345 out of the 615 seats and 38 per cent of the vote. This result boosted the self-confidence of the party and weakened the appeal of coalition. It also shattered the illusion of those sulking senior Conservatives that they were indispensable in an anti-socialist government. They began to contemplate making their peace with the new leadership, even with the upstart Stanley Baldwin when he succeeded Bonar Law as prime minister in May 1923. The election of December 1923 which Baldwin called on a programme of tariff reform finally brought them securely into his net, depriving Lloyd George forever of their political company.

It had also become even more unlikely that he would get much of a welcome from the Labour party. Understandably, they still blamed and distrusted him for the misfortunes suffered by the labour movement and working people during the war and in the post-war depression. But in addition party leaders were also confident by 1922 that their political strategy was correct. They had left Lloyd George's coalition in 1918 and severed the progressive alliance in order to challenge the Liberals for the allegiance of the left, and Labour's progress in parliamentary and local elections had thereafter accelerated. Labour now saw themselves as an alternative party of government and not just as a left-wing pressure group. That their leader, Ramsay MacDonald, was also frightened of Lloyd George's political magic was a further incentive to keep him at arm's length. In the general election of November 1922, Labour won 142 seats, attracted 30 per cent of the vote and became the principal opposition party. Strikingly Labour even won 18 of the 35 seats in Wales. (The Conservatives took 6.) Lloyd George never again could command the principality as a power base. That result was topped in December 1923 when Labour took 191 seats and 31 per cent of the vote: in January 1924 they formed their first, albeit minority, government. Co-operation with Lloyd George looked unnecessary to sustain such an upward curve.

Political necessity therefore drove Lloyd George back into the arms of the Liberal party. His National Liberals were obliged by the break up of the Coalition to contest the general election of 1922 as an independent party. Many candidates faced Conservative and Labour opponents, some even clashed with Independent Liberals, and only 62 out of 162 were successful. However, Asquith's Liberals had done no better, just 54 of their 328 candidates got home. Such results, in the context of massive Conservative and Labour gains, persuaded Lloyd George that only a reunited Liberal party could offer the platform he wanted and a route back to power. While separately the two competing parts were impotent, their combined vote, 29 per cent of the total, suggested real electoral potential. The prospects for a major Liberal recovery appeared obvious, probably within a genuine three-party system. There was no reason for anyone to assume that the Liberals were irrevocably beaten. But reunification would not be automatic or easy. Not only in his private life had Lloyd George been unfaithful, and Asquith, blocking the doorway and wielding his rolling pin, was less forgiving than Margaret. He and his close colleagues were initially very reluctant to welcome back Lloyd George and his supporters.

Two forces effected reunion. Many of the rank and file Liberals had always regretted the split in the historic Liberal party and deplored the way the quarrels of the senior men had damaged party prospects and their own political futures. Moreover, many still admired the energy and originality of Lloyd George, in comparison with Asquith's lack of fizz. But while there were internal pressures encouraging reconciliation, it was largely Baldwin's tariff reform proposals which brought the two sides together in defence of that most ancient of Liberal creeds, free trade. Lloyd George had never been one to bother about status (his taste was for power), and when peace was made in November 1923 he cheerfully acknowledged Asquith as party leader, while rather effacing him by his dynamism during the election campaign. Lloyd George also dipped into the political fund he had accumulated as prime minister to help pay the party's electoral expenses. Liberal candidates contested 453 seats, and Lloyd George buzzed about the country in their support, even appearing sometimes on the same platform as Asquith. They won 159 seats and attracted 30 per cent of the vote, just one point below Labour.

Superficially this was satisfactory. The result apparently demonstrated the success of party unity. It also appeared to confirm the arrival in Britain of three-party politics, with the Liberals holding the balance of power in the new Parliament. However, it was not clear what the Liberals distinctively represented since the election had been fought largely in the defence of free trade, to which Labour was also pledged. Moreover, Liberals were unsure what their future relations with Labour ought to be. Three-party politics posed difficult and divisive problems for the 'piggy-in-the-middle'.

Party leaders, urged on by Lloyd George, agreed that because the electorate had rejected tariff reform Liberals would have to vote with the Labour party in the House of Commons to bring down the Conservative government, and this was accomplished on 21 January 1924. But since Labour held the next largest number of seats, they formed the new government. Lloyd George, supported by most in the party, was at first certain that the Liberal party should give Labour their support. He even expected MacDonald to co-operate with the Liberals in deciding the government's programme. But other Liberals were far less happy about the prospect of backing an ostensibly socialist government. Many reluctantly tolerated Labour in power only because they feared to fight another general election too soon by bringing the ministry down early. The recently restored party unity looked vulnerable to new lines of fracture. Eventually, however, Lloyd George himself lost patience with MacDonald's dogged independence and refusal to co-operate, and it was largely on his insistence that the Liberals combined with Conservatives to vote down Labour's short-lived ministry on 8 October 1924.

This decision led to a general election on 29 October whose consequences were devastating for the Liberal party and ultimately for Lloyd George. The Conservatives promised *not* to introduce tariffs and won a sweeping majority: 419 seats from 48 per cent of the vote. Labour won only 151 seats and lost office, but they had captured 33 per cent of the vote. The Liberals had the resources and the candidates to contest only 340 seats. They attracted nearly 3 million votes, but that was only 18 per cent of the total and they won only 40 seats, including a mere 10 in Wales. Clearly the first-past-the-post electoral system punished them: not surprisingly Liberals agitated for proportional representation.

The humiliation led to bitter recriminations within the party. One response was to blame Lloyd George for not supporting the party adequately from his private political fund. Asquith and his loyalists never quite decided which they resented more: the immoral earnings Lloyd George had made by selling honours as prime minister or his refusal to let them live off the proceeds. Lloyd George regarded his fund as a political asset he was not prepared either to present to former enemies and still resentful 'friends' or to see frittered away in supporting hopeless candidates. The post-election bickering was only submerged by yet more contentious issues, for example when Lloyd George proved to be more sympathetic to the trade unions and hostile to the government during the General Strike in 1926 than either Asquith or Sir John Simon. Amazingly, Asquith even attempted at this time to have Lloyd George dismissed from the party. The supposedly reunited Liberals lacked harmony, and perhaps even any long-term future.

Only one benefit for Lloyd George seemed to flow from the disaster of 1924. Asquith had lost his seat: shortly afterwards he would go to the House of Lords. He was also ageing fast, and many more Liberals recognised his incapacity as party leader. He died in 1928. Meanwhile, Lloyd George was elected chairman of the Liberal parliamentary group in 1924 and acted as the *de facto* party leader, even before taking over the office formally in 1926. In these roles, and still nursing his political fund, Lloyd George set about his last major political crusade. He knew that his return to power was now irrevocably bound up with a recovery of the Liberal party, and he was determined to use the years while the unshiftable Conservative government held office to prepare for the next election.

This required a major overhaul of the party's central and cons- tituency organisation, and he spent lavishly on this business. He also secured Sir Herbert Samuel as a prestigious chairman of the party. The recruiting of more party members and the selection of more parliamentary candidates began to boost morale. The party's publicity operations were extended, pamphlets were printed, party newspapers were launched and teams of lecturers were despatched to address public meetings up and down the country: this was work with which Lloyd George had become familiar before the war. But the crucial task to which he devoted most attention and which drew most deeply upon his experience and political imagination was to define the general politics and the specific policies of the revamped Liberal party

Since being rebuffed by the Conservatives and by Labour, Lloyd George had been thoughtfully seeking a political definition which would legitimise the continued existence of the Liberal party. The trade-union collectivism and professed state socialism of the Labour party had never appealed to him or to the Liberals with whom he must now work. However, he needed to distance himself and the party from the Conservatives with their stern defence of property and their often negative anti-socialism. Nor was it enough merely to describe Liberals in old-fashioned Gladstonian terms as the defenders of free trade, international peace and individual liberties. Instead he proposed to offer the electorate a more positive alternative, a non-socialist but radical centre party. Essentially this meant reviving the New Liberal ideals he and others had embraced before the war, and modernising policies in the light of his wartime experiences and of social and economic conditions in the 1920s.

Others in the party had been thinking on similar lines, particularly intellectuals like Rowntree, Beveridge and Keynes and young members dismayed by the sterility of personality squabbles and the slippage of Liberalism to the margins. At Liberal Summer Schools held from the early 1920s fresh ideas were being explored. Lloyd George identified himself with this rethinking. He lent the discussions his authority and supported detailed investigations with his money. He also added his own ideas. The result was a remarkable sequence of reports, most known as the 'coloured books' from their jacket covers. *Coal and Power* (1924) rejected nationalisation but sought to increase colliery efficiency by state supervised pit closures, amalgamations and better management and to improve working conditions for miners. *The Land and the Nation* (1925) came very close to proposing land nationalisation and suggested state supervision of production in return for financial and technical assistance, security of tenure for farmers and minimum wages and better housing for labourers: echoes here of the pre-war land campaign. *Towns and the Land* (1925) derived from the other part of that earlier exercise and proposed changes in taxation and local rating and more powers for local authorities to build houses and roads and to create open spaces. *Britain's Industrial Future* (1928) offered a constructive alternative to the economic orthodoxy of waiting upon private enterprise and export recovery which it claimed was palpably not tackling either the current economic depression or Britain's long-term economic difficulties. Solutions included public corporations for key industries, state direction of investment into industry, state management of credit plus minimum wages and higher welfare benefits, so as to raise domestic economic demand and profit-sharing. In addition it proposed an immediate programme of state investment in roads, housing, electrification and other public works so as to modernise the nation's infrastructure while providing urgent relief for unemployment. This last aspect was subsequently addressed separately in a widely distributed and much discussed pamphlet boldly entitled *We Can Conquer Unemployment*, issued prior to the general election in 1929.

Lloyd George's plans predictably envisaged an enhanced role for the state. Indeed, their application would have required something like the authority which he had wielded as prime minister in the war, directing labour, instructing private companies, overriding the rights of local authorities and private property owners where they obstructed national needs. The emphasis upon land, both rural and urban, was also predictable, and so too was the interest in minimum wages and other welfare extensions. More original as a response to the prevailing depression was an economic strategy which aimed to steer between state socialism on the one hand and the orthodox reliance on the free market on the other in order to bring to Britain immediate recovery and enhanced prosperity. It is true that some contemporary critics correctly argued that the programme would need a dictatorial central government to direct it, that it would run into practical problems, that it would probably damage the balance of payments and that it would not work upon the economy as quickly or as permanently as claimed. It is also true that some Liberals took fright at what they condemned as socialism and fled to the Conservatives. Nevertheless, the Liberal party and subsequently the electorate were being offered some astonishingly imaginative, radical and yet thoughtfully prepared proposals. No wonder one of Lloyd George's colleagues concluded 'when Lloyd George came back to the party, ideas came back to the party' (quoted in Lucy Masterman, *C.F.G. Masterman*, 1939, pp. 345–6). And he had restored his credentials as a man of the left.

Repairing the party's organisation, defining its political position, drafting its policies and selecting 513 candidates (the largest number since 1910) were supposed to win the general election. Lloyd George had at least ensured that the Liberal proposals largely dominated the election debates, forcing Labour and the Conservatives to respond

74

to his initiatives. But that made the electoral verdict still more bitter. The Liberals won only 59 seats (just 9 in Wales), not much more than in 1924, in spite of their 5.3 million votes, over 23 per cent of the poll. Their MPs were virtually confined to parts of Wales and Scotland, and candidates did particularly badly at the hands of Labour in big cities. The Conservatives gained 38 per cent of the vote and 260 seats. Labour won 37 per cent, 288 seats (25 in Wales), and formed their second government. The election revealed that the Liberal party was in a near terminal decline which not even Lloyd George's policy-making and energetic electioneering could reverse.

One remaining prospect was to try to persuade, or if need be to force, the minority Labour government to implement at least some of his proposals, particularly those directed against unemployment. Labour had pledged themselves to tackle that issue. But in practice the Liberals were largely frozen out by Labour, much as they had been in 1924. Only when unemployment began to soar during 1930 as the world depression began to bite into British exports were some desultory and inconclusive contacts made between Lloyd George and MacDonald. These discussions neither pushed the Labour government towards new economic strategies nor eased the tensions developing within the Liberal party over the proper attitude to be adopted towards Labour. In June 1931 Sir John Simon rejected the party whip and with colleagues began moving towards the Conservatives, trailing behind him, in Lloyd George's choice phrase, 'the slime of hypocrisy'.

Eventually during the summer of 1931 the Labour cabinet failed to agree on cuts in public expenditure and the government split. It was a cruel trick of fate that the normally robust Lloyd George was seriously ill during the critical weeks at the end of July and early August. While doctors operated on his prostate gland and left him to recover, MacDonald was begging for recruits to an all-party National government. There is no doubt that Lloyd George would have agreed to serve. The veteran of coalition could hardly refuse. With his blessing, Sir Herbert Samuel and a few other Liberals joined the ministry on 24 August, but Lloyd George's own last chance of office had gone.

It is, however, doubtful whether he would have stayed long. Lloyd George had accepted the formation of a National government because MacDonald had claimed that it would be just a temporary creation to tackle the immediate emergency. The Conservative members saw it, however, as an opportunity to capitalise on the crisis by calling a general election. Lloyd George was appalled. He was still more upset when Samuel and his band of Liberals chose to remain in the government, ostensibly to preserve national unity. But the unity of the Liberal party was irrevocably shattered. In the election held on 27 October, the Labour party in opposition slumped to 52 seats while for the government the Conservatives won 473, National Labour 13, Sir John Simon's Liberal Nationals 35 and Sir Herbert Samuel's official Liberals 33. Standing outside all this were Lloyd George and his Independent Liberals, a bizarre collection of just four, including his son and daughter. Most of Samuel's Liberals joined them when the National government abandoned free trade and adopted tariffs and imperial preferences in 1932, but the historic Liberal party still looked defunct.

The rest of Lloyd George's career may legitimately be told in brief for henceforth his political impact was negligible. Age was catching up on him, his health was less secure. It is true that in 1935 he launched through the Council of Action for Peace and Reconstruction a revamped version of his unemployment proposals, but he merely hoped that the campaign might influence the policies of others. National government ministers condescended to listen to his proposals, but he could hardly hope to persuade such combined enemies as MacDonald, Baldwin and Neville Chamberlain. The Liberal party fought only 161 seats in the general election that year and won only 20. Thereafter Lloyd George became more preoccupied with foreign affairs. His commentaries made interesting reading in the newspaper columns he took to writing but they had no influence on the course of events. He met and apparently was impressed by Adolf Hitler in 1936. Germany's grievances, Lloyd George agreed, should be fairly addressed. However, he later denounced Chamberlain for his lack of preparedness for war and urged a closer defensive relationship with the Soviet Union. Something of his former concern with national security was evident. But he became increasingly pessimistic, particularly after the outbreak of war, with the capacity of the nation's leaders. Churchill half seriously considered him for a wartime post, perhaps as ambassador in Washington, but such gestures were largely attempts to negate the defeatism he seemed to be spreading. It was perhaps a kindness that by then few were taking him seriously.

Why could Lloyd George not resurrect the Liberal party? Several explanations may be offered. For example, it is probable that the prolonged split in the party from 1916 and the bickering within the leadership even after supposed reunion had damaged electoral confidence in the party. The press, ever liking the personal story, made much of these tensions. But too much can be made of party divisions, which sometimes followed rather than caused defeats and disappointment. Moreover, the Conservative and Labour parties in their time also suffered massive fractures and yet staged successful recoveries.

More serious was the lack of room in the centre ground which Lloyd George's Liberalism was trying to occupy. The Conservatives had shaken off after the war some of the intemperate extremism which had alienated electors; they adopted a sober patriotism and a flexibility over imperial issues which impressed even some Liberals, and they extended (particularly under Neville Chamberlain's direction) the welfare legislation which New Liberalism had launched before the war. The party therefore appeared a respectable and even liberal home for former Liberal voters looking for an effective opposition to the Labour party. At the same time, reasonable observers, including many former Liberal supporters, recognised that the Labour party was not run by Bolsheviks but by sensitive Nonconformists and patriotic trade union leaders. Moreover, Labour policies on free trade, social welfare, taxation, land reform and disarmament were true descendants of Liberal progressivism.

In addition there were long-term social and economic trends over which political parties had little control but which in conjunction with political events reduced Liberalism's former natural supporters. Religious and cultural divisions in the United Kingdom had formerly been expressed in the conflict between Liberal and Conservative parties, giving each much of their purpose and appeal. But Nonconformism was no longer the force it had once been, even in Wales: chapel attendance had peaked before the First World War and the former passion had since been dissipated, perhaps because of the satisfaction of certain issues, perhaps following the sobering experience of the Western front. The nationalism of Wales and of Scotland was also muted. Great Britain had become culturally more united; provincialism no longer demanded the political expression which the Liberal party had formerly offered. Instead, overriding such concerns was a greater awareness of social class, developing particularly in the great cities and in larger factories and mines. Class conflict was heightened by the tensions caused by war and post-war economic depression. This social divide threatened Liberal emphases on shared community values; class found its expression

77

through trade unions and the Labour party on the one hand and the Conservative party representing social stability and property on the other. The efforts of Lloyd George and his colleagues to seek a middle way were crushed between these forces.

There remained little for him to do but to tidy up his past. He had finalised his version of his war record in the extensive memoirs he had written during the 1930s. (He had much enjoyed refighting campaigns against the real enemy: British generals and politicians.) In 1941 his wife Margaret died. His grief reflected his love and perhaps his guilt. Two years later, to the distress of his family and many of his friends, he married his mistress, Frances Stevenson. And in September 1944 he travelled from Bron-y-de, his home at Churt in Surrey where he had lived since 1922, to Ty Newydd, the house and farm he had bought above Llanystumdwy. This was ostensibly a visit, but he seemed to know he was back in Wales to die. One last bizarre gesture; he accepted a peerage in the New Year's Honours list of 1945. Such had been the decline of Liberalism that it was thought likely he would lose the parliamentary seat he had held since 1890. At least he acknowledged that a seat in the Lords was second best. It was an unnecessary manoeuvre. He died on 26 March 1945 and was buried beneath a large boulder beside the Afon Dwyfor in his boyhood village.

Epilogue

Although news of Lloyd George's death was greeted with respectful tributes from most parts of the political spectrum, his personal and political reputation had by then sunk a long way below that which he had enjoyed as 'The People's Champion' in 1909-11 or as 'The Man Who Won the War' in 1918. It might be suggested that his origins explain this lack of security in public affections. Kenneth Morgan has properly emphasised that Lloyd George was by birth, education and Welsh upbringing a political outsider. The argument that this accounts for the hostility he generated must not, however, be exaggerated. The political system in the modern period has been remarkably open to mavericks. Several politicians have reached the top of the greasy pole who have not been standardised Anglo-Saxon, university-educated sons of the English middle class or aristocracy. They range from George Canning, son of an actress, to John Major, son of a trapeze artist, and include an anglicised Jew in Disraeli, a Canadian-Scot in Bonar Law, the illegitimate son of a Scottish domestic servant in Ramsay MacDonald and, of course, Margaret Thatcher, a grocer's daughter. Being a Welsh outsider did, however, make Lloyd George disrespectful of the orthodoxies of English political life into which he crashed: he was intolerant of class conventions and the prestige of the aristocracy, monarchy and even the civil service. It is appropriate that when in his semi-retirement at Churt he became a farmer, specialising in developing types of soft fruit, he should have given the world the 'Lloyd George raspberry'.

However, he failed to retain public approval for more profound reasons. His personal behaviour generated disquiet. His sexual athleticism was perhaps politically least damaging, thanks to a discretion by many parties unlikely to be exercised today. He also managed to disguise his religious doubts at a time when such things mattered, particularly in Wales. But he earned over the Marconi case an unappealing reputation for financial malpractice which the sale of political honours sadly sustained. Several of his cronies were of doubtful virtue. Moreover, his style of political negotiation ultimately generated suspicion, for an element of deception was sometimes later revealed or a worrying contrast between his private talk and his public speech.

Obviously his dislike for the rigidities of party politics aroused much hostility. As a backbencher he had been a rebel. Yet more disturbing was his preference for coalition, not just when waging war but for tackling what he regarded as the equally pressing emergencies of peace. After the Armistice in particular he regarded ancient party structures founded on nineteenth-century principles and conflicts as inappropriate to the new world, a view shared by others in Britain and, for example, in Germany and Italy. Of course, many Liberals were particularly aghast at his disloyalty and blamed him for their party's political decline. He refused to regard the Liberal party as an object of reverence but treated it simply as a vehicle to carry him to destinations; if he saw what he thought was a faster bus he was tempted to hop on. It is ironic that when, for lack of choice after 1922, he was most dedicated to the party it drove him into a cul-de-sac. Politicians, and history, are often most unforgiving of perceived traitors to their party, as Ramsay MacDonald and David Owen were also to discover. (It took a remarkable man with remarkable luck in remarkable circumstances to skip successfully back and forth like Churchill.) Yet the record clearly shows that the splits in the Liberal party owed at least as much to Asquith and later to Simon as to Lloyd George. In any case long-term social and economic factors were probably easing the Liberal party inevitably towards the margins even without their combined help. Indeed, a better case can be made for Lloyd George's huge contribution to sustaining the Liberal party for so long, first as the most conspicuous, consistent and effective New Liberal before the war and then for his restoration of party morale, if not ultimately of party seats, with his revived radical programme during the 1920s.

His background, personal behaviour and political irreverence did not, of course, prevent Lloyd George from achieving political success and from attracting for many years the admiration of a wide range of people and interest groups. Even in opposition during the first part of his career he soon captured the political limelight and gained a loyal following; as a minister and ultimately as prime minister his domination of British politics was by many warmly welcomed; even after 1922 he still retained for a while the capacity to excite and attract not just popular audiences but also discerning intellectuals like Keynes, Rowntree and Beveridge. Clearly this man had redeeming characteristics which help explain his achievements.

Many of those who had business with him reported the potency of his personal charm. Much political business, particularly as Lloyd George liked to conduct it, was handled in personal and private discussion, for example with colleagues in cabinet or with delegations visiting him as a minister. Lloyd George had a remarkable capacity to generate, if he wished, a warm and relaxed atmosphere, highly conducive, for example, to easing the suspicion of trade unions or of Anglican ministers or for reconciling with his wishes the self-interest of insurance companies or munitions manufacturers. The same technique or occasionally its opposite – the controlled explosion of anger – was employed in his conduct of international diplomacy. Personal meetings were also his chosen method for gathering information: his reluctance to read ministerial papers has been grossly exaggerated, but certainly he preferred face-to-face discussions and could grasp essentials with impressive speed.

At the same time he was the most arresting orator of his day. Effective though he often was in the House of Commons, he was usually more persuasive on the public platform, speaking to thousands in unamplified public halls or to yet larger crowds in the open air. He knew the virtue of these occasions in a still raw democratic society, reaching personally to mass audiences and to yet larger sections of the electorate through the press reports he took pains to provide. Many of these speeches were carefully composed. He was in fact almost the last master of a British political tradition which gave way later in his career to the quieter tones of Baldwin, to the radio talk and to the filmed party political broadcast.

What excited many listeners was Lloyd George's ability to describe in graphic terms those national problems which, he said, demanded solutions – for example, the Anglican Church in Wales, the illegitimate privileges of the aristocracy and the House of Lords, the unjust war in South Africa, the just war in Europe, the state of education, rural distress and urban poverty,

81

the waste of unemployment. But more excitingly, he expressed boundless confidence that problems could be solved, and he inspired others with his certainty. He shared to the full the classic Liberal optimism of the nineteenth century, that there really were solutions to all difficulties which well-intentioned men would find; more amazingly, he retained that confidence into the bruising twentieth century. Politics was for Lloyd George the pursuit of the practical, and success was to be measured substantially by legislation and administrative effectiveness. And certainly his record as a minister was outstanding. Quite properly, in later life, while he viewed with pride his brave stand against the Boer War, he derived most inspiration from his accumulation of constructive experiences, first at the Board of Trade, then as a social reforming chancellor and finally as the man who mobilised the nation for war.

Does this sequence demonstrate at least some continuity in Lloyd George's political career? John Grigg and Martin Pugh have argued that even as a novice politician he was never merely a Welsh radical, indifferent to wider British and British Empire concerns, who only later extended his horizons. It also seems that many in Wales became disaffected when they realised how uncommitted he really was to purely Welsh affairs. The phase as the 'Welsh Parnell' disguised even then some lurking wider interests. Moreover, the uneasy relationship he often had with other Liberal radicals may have stemmed from his close identification with them on domestic matters while he was often more aggressive and even illiberal in his approach to external issues, including Ireland. But these distinctions became seriously apparent only during and after the First World War, which seems seriously to have altered his concerns. Too many Liberals, he then claimed, were irresponsibly blind to changing needs. He regarded with contempt those who refused to adapt, often for reasons of ideological consistency, to the world which the war had brought in. He denounced doctrinaires as 'the vultures of principle. They feed upon principle after it is dead.' Circumstances, he claimed, had altered his priorities, but this saddled him with a reputation for inconsistency among less flexible colleagues.

One other discontinuity should be emphasised since it also helps explain his rapid decline in popular esteem. Before the war he had obviously not viewed with indifference or with favour the emergence of the Labour party, and he had been cold towards the collectivist ideals of trade unionism. But he had been confident that the labour movement could be contained within a progressive alliance which the Liberals would securely dominate. His principal targets remained the social, economic and clerical privileges defended by the Conservative party. However, he lost confidence in the efficacy of progressivism and containment when the war appeared to stimulate a dangerous and destabilising militancy among workers in Britain and indeed throughout Europe. Labour's rejection of the Coalition was the last straw. Consequently, his vigorous anti-socialism and his hostility towards post-war strikers, especially miners, marked a real, though he would claim justified, shift in his political responses. His status as a man of the left was thereafter very difficult to restore.

A strong element of continuity may be seen, however, in his early and growing conviction that in a modern society the state ought to assume far greater responsibilities for economic prosperity and social welfare. In this respect he was soon detached from traditional Liberal individualism. But he did not embrace instead old-fashioned Tory paternalism. The obligations upon the state were to extend and protect social rights, particularly civic and political equality and the prosperity and basic social security of the people: safe upon that foundation, people should be free to build their own lives through their own exertions. In return, however, the people had obligations in a democratic society to co-operate with the state in the defence of society's general interests. In Lloyd George's eyes this ultimately legitimised wartime conscription, mobilisation, the hounding of conscientious objectors and limitations on individual civil liberties. But it also provided the ideological underpinning of compulsory state social insurance against sickness and unemployment, old age pensions, council housing, state support for British industry and commerce, state assistance for agriculture, state management of credit and national investments, public corporations and public works as a response to unemployment. It also justified earnings- and wealth-related direct taxation, penalties upon unearned incomes and a fiscal strategy promoting progressive wealth redistribution. These were the themes which Lloyd George began to define as a backbencher, implemented at the Board of Trade, as Chancellor of the Exchequer, as a minister during the war and as prime minister, and finally further refined when out of office from 1922.

His policies may be best characterised as authoritarian: government of the people, for the people but not necessarily by the people. This becomes more evident if we remember his deteriorating interest in Parliament. As a backbencher he had employed the House of

Commons as a public platform, but he had never been deceived into believing that an applauded speech necessarily accomplished much in practice. As a minister and particularly as prime minister he used his executive power to get things done, and regarded the House of Commons as a distraction whose approval he unfortunately had periodically to secure. As noted, he preferred to seek popular support via public speeches and the newspaper press, and he rather disliked having to woo parliamentary consent by chatting up MPs in the House of Commons tearoom. Notoriously, he built up the power of the cabinet office and especially of his prime ministerial office. This personalised authoritarian style of government was characteristic of a number of post-war governments, and it is not surprising that in this respect he admired not only Franklin Roosevelt but also Adolf Hitler: both men seemed to him leaders of strong governments who tackled with energy the domestic problems with which orthodox politicians had merely fiddled.

Another more recent example is Margaret Thatcher: her governments were also characteristically authoritarian, she too was sceptical of the established civil service, she too built up a powerful private office and she too ran her administrations in presidential style. The comparison with Thatcher has a further value. Much of what she attempted to obliterate in her radical governments during the 1980s derived from Lloyd George's legacy. Her emphasis upon private enterprise and self-help challenged his emphasis upon the role of the state as an economic manager and upon its centrality for social welfare. Her task was daunting because what had been developed from his policies had by then become entrenched as the established orthodoxy. Conservative and Labour administrations, even those led by Baldwin between the wars and especially that led by Attlee after the Second World War, had largely followed his leads towards the mixed economy and the welfare state. Contributory state insurance, state involvement in industry, even state support for the revival and modernisation of agriculture owed much to his example. Of course, there were other forces at work and other actors (many like Keynes, Rowntree and Beveridge at various times working colleagues of Lloyd George) in the evolution of these policies, and in detail important deviations can be detected. Biography always runs the risk of exaggerating its subject's influence. Nevertheless, it is reasonable to claim that Lloyd George drafted much of the political agenda for his contemporaries and for his successors. The programme he initiated remained largely unchallenged for at least half a century.

Further reading

An excellent review of the extensive literature has been provided by Chris Wrigley, 'David Lloyd George 1863–1945', *The Historian*, no. 26, Spring 1990, pp. 10–12, published by the Historical Association: this should especially be consulted for specific topics. Among the many biographies the best are Kenneth Morgan, *Lloyd George*, Weidenfeld & Nicolson, London, 1974, short, illustrated and emphasising his Welsh roots; Martin Pugh, *Lloyd George*, Longman, London, 1988, also short, scholarly and boldly setting him within a tradition of centre politics; John Grigg, three volumes so far, published by Methuen, London, *The Young Lloyd George*, 1973, *Lloyd George: The People's Champion 1902–1911*, 1978 and *Lloyd George: From Peace to War 1911–1916*, 1985, in aggregate long, but scholarly, politically astute and immensely readable; Peter Rowland, *Lloyd George*, Barrie & Jenkins, London, 1975, comprehensive and long. The first volume of another huge biography taking his career to 1912 is B.B. Gilbert, *David Lloyd George: A Political Life*, Batsford, London, 1987, massively researched and on some topics fresh in detail and interpretation. The last stages are sympathetically reviewed in a scholarly way in Kenneth Morgan, *Consensus and Disunity: The Lloyd George Coalition Government 1918–1922*, Clarendon Press, Oxford, 1979 and in John Campbell, *Lloyd George: The Goat in the Wilderness 1922–1931*, Cape, London, 1977. Lloyd George's Welsh background is marvellously analysed in chapters of Kenneth Morgan, *Rebirth of a Nation: Wales 1880–1980*, Oxford

University Press, Oxford, 1981. The political history of Britain in his lifetime is discussed in Martin Pugh, *The Making of Modern British Politics 1867–1939*, Blackwell, Oxford, 1982 and more briefly in Glyn Williams and John Ramsden, *Ruling Britain: A Political History of Britain 1688–1988*, Longman, London, 1990. The electoral statistics cited in this study are mainly taken from David Butler and Anne Sloman, *British Political Facts 1900–1979*, Macmillan, London, 1980: other sources slightly differ. A short introduction to one complex issue is Paul Adelman, *The Decline of the Liberal Party 1910–1931*, Longman, London, 1981. Finally, some revealing and entertaining private Lloyd George material has been published: Kenneth Morgan (ed.), *Lloyd George: Family Letters 1885–1936*, University of Wales Press and Oxford University Press, Cardiff and London, 1973; A.J.P. Taylor (ed.), *Lloyd George: A Diary by Frances Stevenson*, Hutchinson, London, 1971 and A.J.P. Taylor (ed.), *My Darling Pussy: The Letters of Lloyd George and Frances Stevenson*, Weidenfeld & Nicolson, London, 1975.